SARISKA
NATIONAL PARK

"Freely the sun gives all his beams to wake
The lotus slumbering in the darkened lake;
The moon unasked expends her gentle light,
Wooing to bloom her lily of the night;
Unasked the cloud its watery burden gives,
The noble nature in benificence lives;
Unsought, unsued, not asking kindness back
Does good in secret for that good's sole sake."

From The *Śatakatrayam* of Bhartrihari, translation of Sri Aurobindo, in A.N.D. Haksar, *A Treasury of Sanskrit Poetry* (Delhi: Shipra Publications, 2002).

SARISKA National Park

Himraj Dang

Published by
INDUS PUBLISHING COMPANY
FS-5, Tagore Garden, New Delhi-110027
Tel.: 25151333, 25935289
mail@indusbooks.com
www.indusbooks.com

ISBN 81-7387-177-9

Printed at
B.B.N. Printers, Najafgarh Road Indl. Area, New Delhi

Preface

A lead article in *The Indian Express* earlier this year (22nd Jan.) asks, 'Have you seen a tiger at Sariska since June? If yes, you're the only one.' The article mentions that no tigers have been seen at Sariska since the last summer, a fact confirmed by park authorities. Further, there is no evidence of pugmarks, kills, or even tiger carcasses. Leopards are now seen frequently where tigers were seen on a daily basis in winters past.

The annual tiger count is admittedly a crude measure of the ecological health of Sariska. While we speculate on what has happened to the 15 tigers seen in the summer (down from 24 in the last census), the park authorities are doing their best to come up with a suitable explanation.

As this situation develops, we cannot but conclude that this ecologically rich but highly stressed park is under severe human pressure from all sides and within. Whether the tiger becomes extinct at Sariska now or later, it is only a matter of time. More importantly, the ecosystem has fragmented and weakened towards collapse, and the park has but a few islands to show what once existed and what can be revived; these fragments no longer constitute a functioning whole.

Serious measures, requiring the support of all agencies of

government to the beleaguered Forest Department, are now needed to nurse the forests back to health. All concerned know these must include the generous and participatory resettlement of insular villages, highly overdue settlement of park boundaries and consequent park notification, improvement of access and departmental control, the launch of a system of buffer zone management/eco-development, and regulation of tourist and local traffic.

This is the only benefit from the demise of the tiger at Sariska (whether real or apparent)—such a development can give the needed impetus for radical measures to revive and strengthen the park, so the Aravalli flora and fauna survive into the distant future.

Himraj Dang

Acknowledgement

Many people have helped with the writing of this book. I would like to acknowledge the contribution of my father Hari Dang, for his inspiration and support for the idea of writing as a discipline, and this book on Sariska in particular. He has been a companion and guide on numerous trips to Sariska and the Haryana Aravallis. The development projects he has established in the areas around Thana Ghazi have been as instructive as they have no doubt been useful to the local communities. My mother Renuka was an old Sariska aficionado and we shared many trips to the park with her in the winter months, including a trip during her long convalescence. My brother Rupin and I have explored Sariska together as we were growing up, as here was a park that was more tractable than the others. His photographs (Nos. 5, 6, 8, 9, 10, 11, 13, 14, 15, 16, 17, 18, 19, 20, 21, 22, 23, 24, 26, 27, 28, 29, 31, 32), selected with Vibha's help, have helped bring out this book.

K.L. Saini's love for Sariska has been infectious. He has been a profound influence in crying for Sariska's upgradation. Dr. Alan Rodgers showed us the way to Keraska and

Umri in his Land Cruiser many years ago, and so we learnt of the floral connections between Africa and Asia. I would also like to thank M.S. Rana at WII library in Dehradun. Pankaj Roy at IJSD in Gurgaon and Nishant Pagare at WFIL have also been of great help.

And, last but not least, Ahilya and Aranya, who have acquired a fondness for this dry and superficially tame Aravalli landscape. And Anisha herself, companion and dear friend in Sariska and so many beautiful places...

HIMRAJ DANG

Contents

List of Illustrations

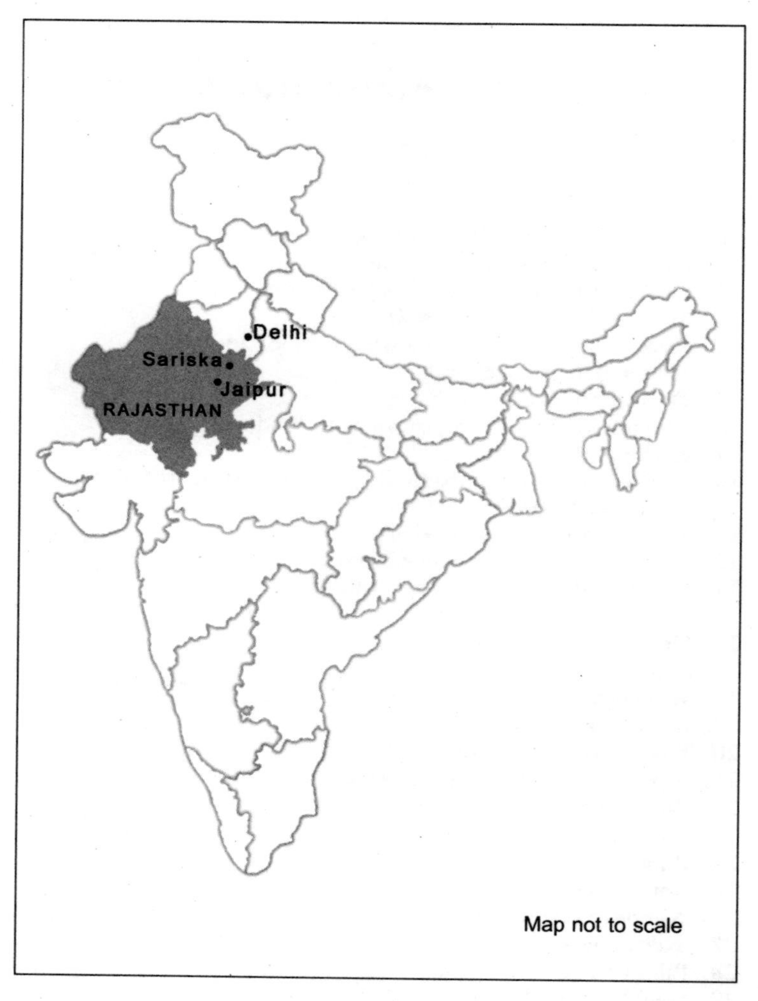

Location map of Sariska National Park

1

Sariska National Park

Physical Features

Sariska National Park and Sanctuary (76°17′-76°34′ N and 27°5′-27°33′ E) is located in the Aravalli mountain range in the district of Alwar, Rajasthan. This area bears the Indian biogeographic definition of 4B—Semi-Arid Gujarat-Rajwara (Rodgers and Panwar, 1988). The forested portion of the Aravallis, which provides a check to the expansion of the Thar desert into fertile Indo-Gangetic plains, has now reduced to 6000 sq km from 40,000 sq km in 1947. When afforded protection, these semi-arid forests can support high ungulate populations and exhibit rich predator diversity.

The highest point in the Aravallis is Mt. Gurushikhar near Mt. Abu (1722 m). The Sariska Aravallis are predominantly made of flat-topped Alwar quartzite, with valleys comprising of Ajaibgarh phyllites. Apart from Sariska, other Aravalli forests which are protected in Rajasthan include Raoli Todgarh, Kumbalgarh, Mt. Abu, and Jaisamand. Sariska is the only large patch of forest left in the northern Aravallis.

Almost all of Sariska is hilly terrain dominated by the Aravallis, which run north-south along the park (and in a SW-NE direction across the state of Rajasthan). The Aravalli mountains at Sariska are topped by two vast plateaux (5 km wide)—Kankwari and Keraska. The park itself varies in altitude from 270 to 722 m.

There are three large lakes in the boundary of the park—Mangalsar (also called Mansarovar), Siliserh, and Somasagar. There are numerous permanent sources of water maintained in the park. These include Bandipul, Pandupol, Tuda, Taraunda, Udainath, Narayani and Talvriksh. Additionally, there are wells at Isawala, Nabawala, Slopka, Kalighati, Taraunda, Sariska, Kankwari and Ganka. The entire area is settled with villages and *guadas* or cattle camps.

The scarcity of perennial water sources at Sariska has prompted successive park administrations to provide water to animals in the summer months. Over the years, this has sustained high levels of ungulate populations. Water is supplied over a broad area of the central valley of the park. Waterholes which are externally supplied are typically located close to forest posts or *chaukis* at Bandipul, Kalighati, Siliberi, Ghamori, Taraunda, Phantakipal, Kankwari, Nilka and Basantpura. Additionally, the construction of anicuts, such as at Brahmnath, have also proved successful in supporting animals in summer. Most of these waterholes have traditionally been provided beside the main road between the park headquarters and Pandupol, since this corridor affords high visibility and presence of animals.

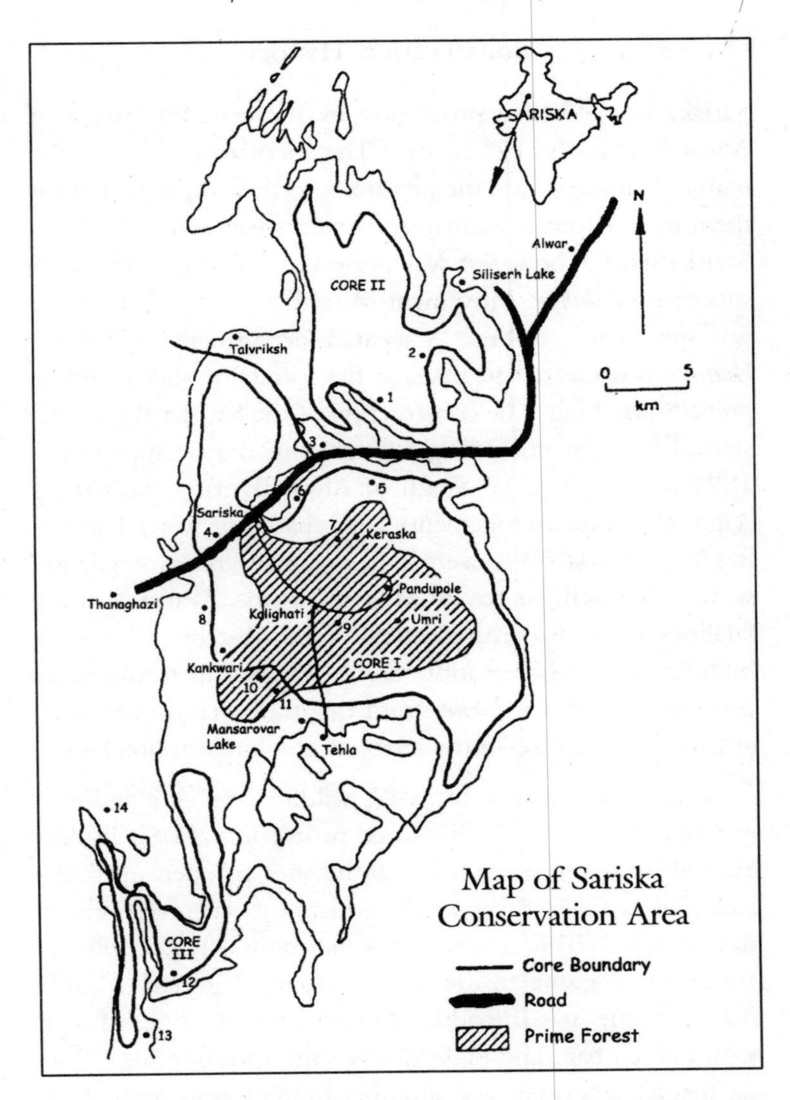

Map of Sariska Conservation Area

Index of Place Names

1. Raika
2. Kalikhol
3. Kushalgarh
4. Bandipul
5. Naldeshwar
6. Bhartrihari
7. Algual
8. Udainath
9. Slopka
10. Rajoregarh
11. Neelkanth Mahadev
12. Narayani Mata
13. Bhangarh
14. Ajaibgarh

Conservation History

Sariska was afforded protection by the erstwhile rulers of Alwar state in the 19th century. The abundance of game, the natural landscape, and the proximity to their capital attracted them to this forest. Human settlements were removed from Sariska itself. The forest was preserved exclusively for royal shooting or *shikar*. Movement of traffic and even of people was subject to a toll tax. A separate department—the *shikar khana*—was created to manage the forest for shikar and to prevent poaching. The construction of the Sariska Palace was started by Maharaja Mangal Singh, but only completed in 1894 by Maharaja Jai Singh of Alwar. During the latter's reign, elaborate arrangements were made for water harvesting in the forest. Wells were dug, streams were dammed, and water channelized to suitable locations. Water storage facilities were also created at this time. Watch towers were built for wildlife observation. Some of the *shikar* trophies and photographs of old *shikars* from this time may still be seen at the Sariska Palace—now restored as a modern hotel.

After Independence in 1947, wildlife was shot indiscriminately for crop and livestock protection. Local leaders exerted great pressure on the authorities to open up fertile valley lands for settlement. The sanctuary was given protection in 1955. This resulted in some modest restrictions on shooting of game inside the sanctuary. Limited wildlife management was introduced—restricted to 'tiger shows' with buffalo bait, and night drives with 'spot-lighting.' Even so, neither was organized shooting in the forests around the sanctuary stopped, nor was human settlement in the neighbouring fertile valleys curtailed.

When Project Tiger was launched in 1973, Sariska was unfortunately not included in the nine parks that were initially chosen. By this time, unrestricted grazing was taking place throughout the park. Unpalatable weeds like *Adhatoda vasica* (locally known as 'Bansa') and *Cassia tora* had replaced fodder grass in most affected areas. The cattle, coming from insular villages, as well as from outside the sanctuary, brought in communicable diseases. Most of the sanctuary's 'sambhar' population was wiped out in 1971 by a major epidemic. In the absence of any water management, the perennial scarcity of water became a major limiting factor for animal populations. Visiting Baoria tribals joined hands with the insular villagers to help kill crop-raiding animals. Man-made fires to improve grazing for cattle became common. The failed attempt to move out villages in 1976 (some villages moved out, claimed compensation, and then returned) hampered any effort at change (and this has continued to be the major obstacle to conservation at Sariska).

With this litany of problems, the park was thankfully brought under Project Tiger in the second phase of the Project's expansion in 1978-79, as the north-west limit of the tiger's distribution. The park now includes the old *shikar* forests of Alwar state nestled in the Aravalli range. Central assistance under Project Tiger is used for habitat improvement, creation of waterholes, and additional protection. Threats to the tiger (and key mammal prey species) remain—loss and fragmentation of habitat, poaching, retaliatory destruction by cattle owners, illegal cutting for firewood, and illegal grazing. To this end, an integrated eco-development project with funding of Rs. 1.6 crore is under implementation. The idea behind this is to help protect the buffer by involving villagers in development projects.

While the central area of Sariska has now benefited from improved conservation inputs, chiefly cattle management, provision of water, and modest restriction of temple and truck traffic through the park, the peripheral areas (including two out of three Core Areas) and those areas disturbed by villages located inside the park, continue to suffer. The central valley shows significantly higher populations of more sensitive herbivores like 'cheetal' and 'sambhar' than ever before, and a decline in the relative proportion of 'nilgai'. This situation results from improved availability and quality of fodder, and restriction of cattle grazing in many areas. Successive park administrations should be complemented for this visible and significant improvement in wildlife populations in this limited area.

The protected area at Sariska is all of 492 sq km (the Sanctuary notified in 1959), 293 sq km of which was indicated for grant of National Park status in 1982 (the final notification has still not been executed). The total forest area brought under Project Tiger in 1979 is 866 sq km (split into a Core zone of 497 sq km and a Buffer zone of 369 sq km). Given the earlier figures for the sanctuary and park status, much of forest area under Project Tiger has still not been accorded full Protected Area (PA) status. Since 1982, the national park proposal is pending identification of boundaries and settlement of rights of the villages within the boundaries of the notified area.

The 37 forest blocks at Sariska are administered in 4 ranges and 75 beats—Sariska (205 sq km), Tehla (341 sq km), Akbarpur (219 sq km) and Talvriksh (101 sq km). There are three Core Areas at Sariska where removal of firewood and grass are supposed to be prohibited. Core Area One (274 sq km) comprises the central section from Thana Ghazi to Baran Tal gate, including Kalighati, Kankwari, Udainath, Naldeshwar, Pandupol, Siliberi, Umri, Ganka, Duhar Mala, Sukola, and Devri. This section roughly corresponds with the future national park, where no habitation is legal. There are 12 villages located in this section. Core Area Two includes the Reserved Forests of Kalikhol, Raika Mala, and Panidhal. Core Area Three covers the forests of Mala Kishori, Selibawri, Ajaibgarh, Bhangarh, Narayaniji Parashar and Koh, adjacent to the heavily mined areas to the south-west of the park. Degrading forests still extend from this section through the fertile Jagannanthpura valley to the Jamwa-Ramgarh Sanctuary.

Tourism

The close proximity of the park to Delhi, which is 163 km away, is a tremendous advantage for tourism. Alwar town, which is a district headquarters, and increasingly host to many agro-industrial businesses, is only 37 km away. The park can be accessed from the Delhi-Jaipur highway (NH8) at Shahpura, which is only 44 km away. Jaipur city, the state capital, is located at a distance of 108 km from the park. It is no wonder that various naturalists have visited, and so much has been written about Sariska over the years (Alves, 1998; Breeden, 1996; Dang, 1991a; Israel, 1987; Monga, 2002; Saini, no date; Sharma, 1988; Sharma, 1998; 'Ziddi,' 1998).

Tourist accommodation is principally at Tiger's Den (operated by the Rajasthan Tourism Development Corporation) and the newly refurbished and expanded Sariska Palace. Another new property that has come up near the forest at Thana Ghazi is Tiger Haven. Siliserh Palace Hotel is located by the Siliserh lake at the northern edge of the park—an exquisite princely property, now a shadow of its former opulence under state-owned management.

Apart from the park, the locality has various tourist attractions, more completely described in chapter 5. The temple of Bhartrihari at the south-eastern edge of the park, is famous all over Rajasthan for its fairs and is a center of pilgrimage. It is named after the ancient ruler and sage—Bhartrihari of Ujjain—who realized the folly of material attachments, and renounced his kingdom to devote his time to prayer.

Neelkanth Mahadeva is a ruined temple complex, the ruins of over 300 Hindu and Jain temples constructed between the 8th and 12th centuries. Naldeshwar is a famous local temple located a short walk from the main Alwar-Sariska road. Talvriksh on the northern edge of the park is another center for pilgrimage in Rajasthan.

Near Kankwari fort, on top of the western plateau, where, it is believed Dara Shikoh was imprisoned by Aurangzeb, are the ruined temples of Rajoregarh. Kankwari itself is worth a visit, with its splendid view of the entire hilltop plateau. The Aravalli forest remains on the far hills, but it is retreating fast before the twin threats of grazing and encroachment.

The tourism season at the park is between September and March, when daytime temperatures vary from 16°C to 34°C.

During the winter months, the temperature drops to freezing on occasion. The summer months are extremely hot and dry with daytime temperatures exceeding 48°C. The park is closed during the monsoon, receiving an annual rainfall of 620 mm. Closure does not, unfortunately, stop the plying of buses and the passage of pilgrims to Pandupol year round.

Flora

As per the Champion and Seth classification of vegetation types (1968), Sariska is a prime example of Tropical Dry Deciduous Forest (TDD or category 5). Also present is Tropical Thorn Forest (TTF or category 6). The former category includes Northern Dry Mixed Deciduous Forest (5B/C2 [ii]), Dry Tropical Riverine Forest (4/ISI), *Anogeissus pendula* Forest (5/E1), *Boswellia* Forest (5/E2), *Butea* Forest (5/E5), *Phoenix* Forest (5/E8 [a]), and Dry Bamboo Brakes (5/E9). The latter category includes Thorn Forest (6A/C1. 6B/C2), and Tropical *Euphorbia* Scrub (6E1). Degradational stages of both categories are also prevalent. These subtypes are described in greater detail in Rodgers (1985). The total flora of Sariska would comprise approximately 300 species, reflecting the severity of the dry climate, and the similarity of the few types of vegetation.

As a result of the terrain and the long dry season, water is a limiting factor. Dry and short grass with open woodland comprising trees of 'dhok' (*Anogeissus pendula*), 'churel'/ 'chirol' (*Holoptelia integrifolia*), 'dhak' (*Butea monosperma*), 'khair' (*Acacia catechu*), and 'ber' (*Zizyphus mauritiana*) is the most extensive habitat type, interspersed by well-wooded long low hills with sharp hog-back ridges on all sides. The steep slopes of the hills are drier and are dominated by 'salar' (*Boswellia serrata*), the gum tree or 'keraya' (*Sterculia urens*), with its characteristic white bark, 'dhawa' (*Anogeissus latifolia*), 'tendu' (*Diospyros melanoxylon*), and 'khair' (*Acacia catechu*). These trees are slow-growing and attain modest heights.

Where there is water, there is an abundance of bamboo and 'khajur'. The 'dhok' is the dominant tree-type on the lower slopes, comprising 90 percent of the tree canopy of the park. Its lush green color during the monsoon turns to a burnished red in winter, followed by a drab grey in summer. The tree has a small canopy, but typically the crowns of neighbouring trees touch. The best example of this forest in India is in the precincts of the Bala Qila Fort in Alwar where, in the absence of grazing, the trees have grown to form an impenetrable tree-cover. The 'dhok' tree typically grows to a height of 8-10 m. Bamboo also grows on steep slopes. The valleys are dominated by 'dhak', whose crimson blossoms in March/April are spectacular. Grasslands are dominated by 'ber' and 'khair.'

The stream or *nullah* beds host semi-evergreen vegetation in narrow strips along the *nullahs*. In these strips grow the larger trees at Sariska—'aam' (*Mangifera indica*), 'jamun' (*Syzygium cumini*), 'peepul' (*Ficus religiosa*), 'bargad' (*Ficus benghalensis*), 'guler' (*Ficus glomerata*), 'imli' (*Tamarindus indica*), 'khajur' (*Phoenix sylvestris*), 'lasoda' (*Cordia dichotoma*), 'arjun' (*Terminalia arjuna*) and 'bahera' (*Terminalia behera*). These trees attain larger heights and crowns.

In the lean summer months, the deciduous canopy, principally 'dhok', provides fodder to the herbivores. Additionally, the *Capparis sepiaria* or 'heens' is critical to animal survival in summer (Rodgers, 1990). Coupled with provisioning of water by the park management, these plants allow Sariska to sustain dense prey population nearly comparable to parks with much more rainfall.

Sariska also retains natural water sources in the dry months, such as the perennial Algual spring. Rodgers (1989) has written about the importance of conserving moister valleys and vegetation with permanent water. The evergreen shade and cover host fruit and fodder resources which support a wide variety of mammals and birds in these locales. Even here, though, there is strong evidence of biotic pressures which have inhibited the regeneration of the *Boswellia* on the slopes and fruiting species and 'khajur' in the stream bed. The fact that the tree canopy shows greatest diversity in the middle levels indicates lack of regeneration. Large gaps in the forest continuity, relict trees, and the signs of grazing and lopping, only confirm the poor regeneration and biotic disturbance of the largely evergreen spring forest. Rodgers suggests strong management action to protect such riverine forests by means of removable fencing, plantation and posting of forest guards.

Table 1 gives a representative list of higher plants representing most of the common or characteristic tree, shrub and grass species. The list is large enough to characterize the vegetation in Core Area 1 (see also Parmar, 1985; Rodgers, 1985; Sahni, 1998).

Table 1. Representative list of higher plants

Typical habit of the plant species is indicated (T = Tree, S = Shrub, H = Herb, C = Climber), along with some common local names, which can help in field identification.

Scientific name	Typical habit	Common/local name
Abrus precatorius	C	Chirmi/Murethi
Acacia catechu Wild.	T	Khair
Acacia leucophloea	T	Ronjh
Acacia nilotica (L.) Del.	T	Babul
Acacia seima Kurz	T	
Acacia senegal Wild.	T	Gum Arabic, Kumta
Acanthospermum hispidum DC.	H	
Achyranthes aspera L.	H	Andhijhara
Acrocephalus capitatus Benth.	H	
Actinopteris radita	H	
Adhatoda vasica Nees	H	Bansa/Adus
Adiantum incisum	H	
Adina cordifolia Hook. f.	T	Haldu
Aegle marmelos Corr.	T	Bel
Aerva scandens Wall.	H	
Albizia lebbek Benth	T	Kala Siris
Allium sp.	H	
Amaranthus spinosus	H	Jungli Chaulai
Anisameles ovata R.Br	H	
Anisomales ovata R.Br.	H	
Anogeissus latifolia Wass.	T	Dhawa
Anogeissus pendula Edgw.	T	Dhok/Kardhai
Apluda mutica L.	H	
Aristida funiculata Trin. and Rupr.	H	Lapla
Asparagus racemosus Wild.	C	Naharkata/Satavar
Azadirachta indica L.	T	Neem

Scientific name	Typical habit	Common/local name
Balanites aegyptiaca (L.) Del.	T	Hingu/Hingot
Barleria cristata L.	H	
Barleria prionitis L.	H	
Bauhinia racemosa Lam.	T	Jhinjeri
Bauhinia vareigata	T	Kachnar
Blainvillea rhomboides Cass.	H	
Boerhavia repens L.	H	
Bombax ceiba L.	T	Semul
Boswellia serrata Roxb.	T	Salai
Bothriochloa ischaemum (L.) Keng.	H	
Butea monsperma (Lamk.) Taub.	T	Dhak, Palash
Butea superba Roxb.	C	
Calotropis procera	S	Akada
Capparis decidua (Forsk) Edgw	S, T	Dela/Kair
Capparis sepiaria L.	S	Heens
Capparis zeylanica L.	S	
Cardiospermum helicacabum L.	C	Baloon creeper
Carissa carandas L	S	Karaunda
Caseria tomentosa Roxb.	T	Chilla
Cassia fistula L.	H	Amaltas
Cassia occidentalis	S	Kasondi
Cassia tora	H	Panwar
Cayratia carnosa	C	Ramehana
Celastrus paniculatas Wild.	T	Malkangni
Celosia argentea L.	H	
Cenehrus spp.	H	Anjan
Chloris barbata Sw.	H	
Chloris dolichostachya Laga.	H	
Chrysopogon montanus Trin.	H	
Cleame viscosa L.	H	
Clerodendron phlomidis L.f.	C, S, T	

Scientific name	Typical habit	Common/local name
Clerodendron multitlorum	S	Arni
Cocculus hirustus	C	Pilwani
Commelina kurzii CL.	H	
Commiphora wightii	H'	Gugal
Corcchorous olitorious	H	Sanohari
Cordia dichotoma	T	Lasauda
Cordia obligua Wild	T	Lasauda
Crataeva adansonli DC. subsp. *odora* Jacobs	T	
Crotalaria medicaginea Lam.	H	
Cuscuta reflexa	C	Amarbel/Akashbel
Cymbopogon martinii (Roxb.) Wats.	H	Rosha
Cynodon dactylon	H	Dub
Cyperus compressus L.	H	Motha
Cyperus eleusinoides Kunth	H	
Cyperus tegetiformis Roxb.	H	
Dalbergia lanceolata L.	T	
Dalbergia sissoo Roxb.	T	Sheesham
Datura metel	S	Dhatura
Dendrocalamus strictus (Roxb.) Nees	H	Bans or Bamboo
Desmostachya bipinatta	H	Dab
Dicanthium annulatum Stapf.	H	
Dichrostachys cinera W. & A.	T	Goya Kher
Dicliptera roxburghiana Nees	H	
Diospyros cordifolia	T	Bistendu
Doispyros melanoxylon Roxb.	T	Tendu
Echinochloa colonum L.	H	
Echinops echinatus	H	Untkatalo
Ehretia canarensis	T	Chamaror
Ehretia obtusifolia Hochst.	T	Desi Papri
Elaeodendron sp.	T	

Scientific name	Typical habit	Common/local name
Eleusine indica Gaertn.	H	Jhania
Embilica officinalis (L.)	T	Amla
Eragrostic japonica (Thrub.) Trin.	H	
Eragrostic tenella P. Beauv.	H	Underpooncha Chhota
Erianthemum purpurescens Nees	H	
Erigeron sp.	H	
Euphorbia granulata Forsk.	H	
Euphorbia neriifolia L.	T	Dhudhi
Euphorbia thymipholia	H	Dhudhi
Ficus benghalensis L.	T	Bargad
Ficus glomerata Roxb.	T	Guler
Ficus palmata Forsk	T	Anjir
Ficus racemosa L. var. *typica* Barrett.	T	
Ficus religiosa L.	T	Peepul
Ficus infectoria	T	Pilkhan
Ficus rumphii	T	Parkhad
Ficus tomentosa Roxb.	T	
Fimbristylis stolonifera C.B.CI.	H	
Flacourtia indica (Burn f.) Merr	S	Kandai
Flacourtia sepiaria Roxb.	S	
Fluggea leucopyrus Wild.	S	
Garuga pinnata Roxb.	T	Kharpat
Grewia abutifolia Juss.	T	
Grewia flavescens Juss.	S	
Grewia hainesiana Hole	T	Phalsa
Grewia hirsuta Vahl (+ *G. salvifolia* Heyne)	S	Kala Dhaman
Grewia populifolia Vahl	T	
Grewia tilaefolia Vahl	T	Dhaman
Gymnosporia montana Lawson	T	

Scientific name	Typical habit	Common/local name
Helicteres isora L.	C	Marorphali
Heteropogon contortus Roem. and Schult.	H	Kummeeria
Holarrhena antidysenterica Wall.	S/T	Kura
Holoptelea integrifolia Planch.	T	Chirol/Churel
Ichnocarpus frutescens R.Br	C/S	Dudhi
Imperata cylindrica (L.) P. Beauv	H	
Indigofera cordifolia	H	Bekar
Indigofera crassiodes Roth. & DC.	H	Bekar
Indigofera spicata Forsk. (Jacq.)	H	
Inga dulse	S	Jungle Jalebi
Ipomaea aquatica	H	Nadi
Ipomaea fistulosa	S	Besharam
Ipomoea muricata Jacq.	C	Nishoth
Ipomoea pes-tigridis L.	C	Besharam
Iseilema prostratus	H	Gandhel
Kigelia africana (Lam.) Benth.	T	Sausage tree
Kirganelia reticulate	S	Makhi
Lannea coromandelica (Hout) Merr	T	Jhingan/Gurjan
Lantana camara L. var. *aculeata* (L.) Mold.	H	Lantana
Lawsonia inermis	S	Mehandi
Lemna paucicostata	H	Kai
Leucas mollissima Wall.	H	
Limonia acidissima L.	T	Beli
Ludwigia octovalvis (Jacq.) Raven	H	
Luffa acutangula	C	Kedwai Toria
Maeurua arenaria Hook. f. and Th.	C	
Mallotus philippensis Muel-Arg.	T	Rohini
Mangifera indica L.	T	Aam
Mitragyna parvifolia Korth	T	Kaim/Kalam

Scientific name	Typical habit	Common/local name
Momordiea diorea	C	Kakoda
Moringa oleifera Lamk.	T	Sainjna
Morus alba	T	Shehtoot
Mucuna prurita Hook.	C	Kaunch
Nelumbo nucifera Gaertn.	H	Kamal
Neptunia prostrata	H	Chhui Mui
Nyctanthes arbor-tristis L.	S	Harshringar
Nymphea nocuhalli	H	Kumudini
Nymphea stellate	H	Nili Kumudini
Nymphoides eristatum	H	Kumudini Nanhi
Nymphoides indicum	H	Chhoti Kumudini
Ocimum basilicum L.	H	Tulsi
Oryza spp.	H	Bagrru Dhan
Ougenia oegenesus	T	Sandan
Parkinsonia aculeata L.	T	
Paspalum distichum L.	H	Aineha
Paspalum scrobiculatum	H	Kodra
Pennisetum orirntale Rich.	H	
Peristrophe bicalycalata (Retz.) Nees	H	
Phoenix sylvestris L.	T	Khajur
Pipalia lappacea Juss.	H	
Plumbago zeylanica L.	H	Chitrak
Prosopis cinerarea (L) Druce	T	Sangar, Khejri, Jhand
Prosopis juliflora (sw) DC	T	Vilayti Kikar
Randia dumetorum Lam.	S	Maindal
Randia tetrasperma Benth. and Hook. f.	S	Bhedra
Rhus mysorensis Heyne	S	
Rhynchosia himalensis Benth.	C	
Rivea hypo-cratariformis Choisy.	C	
Saccharum munja	H	Munj

Scientific name	Typical habit	Common/local name
Saccharum spontaneum	S	Kans
Salvadora persica	S	Jal
Salvadora oleoides Dena	S	Pilu
Settaria verticallata (L.) P. Beauv.	H	
Spirodela polyrhiza	H	Kai
Solanum incanum L.	T	
Solanum indicum L.	H	Makoy
Solanum nigrum	H	Makoy
Sorghum halapense (L.) Pers.	H	Barru
Sporobolum marginatus	H	Usari
Sterculia urens Roxb.	T	Keraya
Sterculia villosa Roxb.	T	Godgudala
Stereospermum sauveolens DC.	T	Padal
Syzygium cuminii (L.) Skeels	T	Jamun
Tamarindus indica L.	T	Imli
Tamarisk aphylla	H	Farash
Tecomella undulata (Seem) Sm.	T	Roheda, Rugtrora
Tephrosia hamiltonii	S	Dharmasa
Tephrosia purpurea Pers.	H	Dharmasa
Terminalia arjuna Bedd.	T	Arjuna
Terminalia belerica Roxb.	T	Bahera
Terminalia tomentosa	T	Sahaj/Sadar/Sain
Themeda quadrivalvis O. Ktze.	H	
Tinospora cordiforia	C	Singhi bel/Nimgiloy
Trema politoria Planch	S	Khakshi
Tribuls terrestis L.	H	Gokhru
Trichosanthes cucumerina L.	C	
Tridax procumbens L	H	
Typha angustata	H	Patera
Vetiveria zizanioides	H	Khus
Vicia sp.	H	

Scientific name	Typical habit	Common/local name
Vogelia indica Gibson	S	
Wrightia tinctoria R.Br	T	
Wrightia tomentosa Roem. and Schultes	T	Dudhi
Xanthium strumarium L.	H	
Zizyphus mauritiana Lamk.	T	Ber
Zizyphus nummularia R. and S.	S	Jharber
Wolfia arrhza	H	Kai
Woodfordia fruticosa (L.) Kurz.	S	Dhawai

Fauna

The park supports a diverse set of mammals. Besides the principal predator, the tiger, there are a number of large carnivores including leopard (*Panthera pardus*), hyaena (*Hyaena hyaena*), sloth bear (*Melursus ursinus*), dhole (*Cuon alpinus*), caracal (*Caracal caracal*), and wolf (*Canis lupus*). Smaller carnivores include the jungle cat (*Felis chaus*), Indian fox (*Vulpes bengalensis*), mongoose (*Herpestes* spp.), and ratel (*Mellivora capensis*) (see Table 2 for a list of large mammals; Gujarat Ecological Society, 2003; Menon, 2000).

Till the 1940s, the tiger flourished in all but the extreme western districts of Rajasthan, protected no doubt by the princely states. Since Independence, the tiger has been steadily leaving Rajasthan district by district—Pali in 1970, Mt. Abu in 1971, Jhunjhunu and Sikar in 1976, and Kota (Darrah) and Chittor (Rawatbhata) in 1980 (Soni, 2002). Transients have been seen in Bundi, Jamwa Ramgarh, Darrah and Ramgarh Vishdhari in recent time. Today, the tiger (barely) survives in Rajasthan only in the state's two national parks—Sariska and Ranthambhor. Apparently, the upgradation of Darrah to NP status is imminent. A tiger was recently run over by a train near the Darrah forests.

The principal herbivores the park supports in this habitat are: 'nilgai' (*Bosephalus tragocamelus*) and higher densities of 'sambhar' (*Cervus unicolor*) and 'cheetal' (*Axis axis*), the latter two species preferring the woodland to the grassland. The 'sambhar' is the largest Indian deer and is seen singly or in smaller numbers. The 'cheetal' is most often seen in large herds, feeding on grasses and fallen 'ber' and 'dhok' leaves, often in association with the 'langur' monkey. The 'langur' provides the 'cheetal' with fallen leaves, and both species benefit from each other's alarm calls. Smaller herbivores include the rare 'chausingha' (*Tetraceros quadricorns*) and 'chinkara' (*Gazella bennettii)*, and the more common wild boar (*Sus scrofa*).

The most common primate is the common 'langur' (*Presbytis entellus*), followed by the rhesus monkey (*Macaca mulatta*), both of which are present in large groups at the temple complexes inside the park.

An interesting study was conducted at Sariska in 1992 to study the effects of tree debarking and habitat use by the Indian porcupine (*Hystrix indica*), which is commonly seen at night in the forest (Sharma and Prasad, 1992). The researchers were acting on the concern of the park management that the reduced tree regeneration caused by the high incidence of grazing near villages in the park would be further retarded by the debarking of certain valuable trees by the resident porcupines. After an extensive ecological study across the park, involving the monitoring of 4000 trees, the researchers found that tree debarking was indeed prevalent. However, they concluded that tree debarking did not cause any appreciable tree mortality, and as such did not warrant management intervention. Favoured tree species debarked were *Acacia catechu, A. leuocophlea, Butea monosperma,* and *Zizyphus mauritiana*. Interestingly enough, *Anogeissus pendula, Balanites aegyptica, Boswellia serrata* and *Capparis decidua* were not debarked at all. Such ecological studies should become a routine feature of park management across the country. Unfortunately, most Project Tiger parks have unfilled posts and budgets for resident researchers, and the WII is filling the breach.

Some of the more unique birds at Sariska include the White-backed Vulture, Pallas' Fishing Eagle, Red Spurfowl, Common Sandgrouse, Indian Pitta, and the Great Horned Owl (see Table 3 for a list of representative birds; Ali, 1998; Sankar, 1993). The presence of both species of Spurfowl viz. Red and Painted species, as reported by Sankar in 1993, was a first in Indian ornithology. Of course, both birds are routinely observed in the hill areas.

Sariska is host to a few species of fish as well (Ajith Kumar and Sankar, 1993). While there are no permanent water sources in Sariska proper, there are a number of ephemeral streams and pools. Except for a few natural springs, water in these locations dries up. The common species found in waterbodies in the park are *Noemachilus botia*, *Labio boggut*, *Puntius sarana*, *Garra gotyla* and *Rasbora daniconius*.

Table 2 gives the list of representative large mammals, and Table 3 gives the list of representative birds found in Sariska National Park.

Table 2. Representative list of large mammals

Common name	Scientific name
Caracal	*Caracal caracal*
Chausingha	*Tetracerus quadricornis*
Chinkara	*Gazella bennettii*
Cheetal	*Axis axis*
Small Indian Civet	*Viverricula indica*
Fox	*Vulpes bengalensis*
Hare	*Lepus nigricollis*
Hyaena	*Hyaena hyaena*
Jackal	*Canis aureus*
Jungle Cat	*Felis chaus*
Langur	*Presbytis entellus*
Leopard	*Panthera pardus*
Common Mongoose	*Herpestes edwardsii*
Ruddy Mongoose	*Herpestes smithi*
Nilgai	*Bosephalus tragocamelus*
Palm Civet	*Paradoxurus hermaphroditus*
Pangolin	*Manis crassicaudata*
Porcupine	*Hystrix indica*
Rhesus Macaque	*Macaca mulatta*
Ratel	*Mellivora capensis*
Rusty Spotted Cat	*Prionailurus rubiginosus*
Sambhar	*Cervus unicolor*
Sloth Bear	*Melursus ursinus*
Five-striped Palm Squirrel	*Funambulus pennanti*
Tiger	*Panthera tigris*
Wild Boar	*Sus scrofa*
Wild Dog	*Cuon alpinus*
Wolf	*Canis lupus*

Table 3. Representative list of birds

Common name	Scientific name
Avocet	*Recurvirostra avosetta*
Common Babbler	*Turdoides caudatus*
Jungle Babbler	*Turdoides straitus*
Large Grey Babbler	*Turdoides malcolmi*
Yelloweyed Babbler	*Chrysomma sinense*
Crimsonbreasted Barbet	*Megalaima haemacephala*
Bluecheeked Bee-eater	*Merops superciliosus*
Bluetailed Bee-eater	*Merops philippinus*
Green Bee-eater	*Merops orientalis*
Black Bittern	*Ixobrychus flavicollis*
Chestnut Bittern	*Ixobrychus cinnamomeus*
Little Bittern	*Ixobrychus minutus*
Bittern	*Botaurus stellaris*
Bluethroat	*Erithacus svecicus*
Redvented Bulbul	*Pycnonotus cafer*
Redwhiskered Bulbul	*Pycnonotus jocosus*
Whitecheeked Bulbul	*Pycnonotus leucogenys leucotis*
Blackheaded Bunting	*Emberiza melanocephala*
Crested Bunting	*Melophus lathami*
Greyheaded Bunting	*Emberiza fucata*
Greynecked Bunting	*Emberiza buchanani*
Redheaded Bunting	*Emberiza brunniceps*
Whitecapped Bunting	*Emberiza stewarti*
Dark Grey Bush Chat	*Saxicola ferrea*
Pied Bush Chat	*Saxicola caprata*
Honey Buzzard	*Pernis ptilorhyncus*
Longlegged Buzzard	*Buteo rufinus*
White-eyed Buzzard-eagle	*Butastur teesa*
Brown Rock Chat	*Cercomela fusca*
Collared Bush Chat	*Saxicola torquata*

Common name	Scientific name
Coot	*Fulica atra*
Cormorant	*Phalacrocorax carbo*
Indian Cormorant	*Phalacrocorax fuscicollis*
Little Cormorant	*Phalacrocorax niger*
Coucal	*Centropus sinensis*
Lesser Coucal	*Centropus toulou*
Indian Courser	*Cursorius coromandelicus*
Baillon's Crake	*Porzana pusilla*
Brown Crake	*Amauronis akool*
Ruddy Crake	*Porzana fusca*
Spotted Crake	*Porzana porzana*
Common Crane	*Grus grus*
Demoiselle Crane	*Anthropoides virgo*
Sarus Crane	*Grus antigone*
Spotted Grey Creeper	*Salpornis spilonotus*
House Crow	*Corvus splendens*
Jungle Crow	*Corvus macrorhynchos*
Indian Cuckoo	*Cuculus micropterus*
Pied Crested Cuckoo	*Clamator jacobinus*
Sirkeer Cuckoo	*Taccocua leschenaultii*
Blackheaded Cuckoo-shrike	*Coracina melanopetra*
Large Cuckoo-shrike	*Coracina novaehollandiae*
Stone Curlew	*Burhinus oedicnemus*
Darter	*Anhinga rufa*
Indian Ring Dove	*Streptopelia decaocto*
Little Brown Dove	*Streptopelia senegalensis*
Red Turtle Dove	*Streptopelia tranquebarica*
Rufous Turtle Dove	*Streptopelia orientalis*
Spotted Dove	*Streptopelia chinensis*
Ashy Drongo	*Dicrurus leucophaeus*
Black Drongo	*Dicrurus adsimilis*
Whitebellied Drongo	*Dicrurus caerulescens*

Common name	Scientific name
Comb Duck	*Sarkidiornis melanotos*
Spotbill Duck	*Anas poecilorhyncha*
Tufted Duck	*Aythya fuligula*
Dunlin	*Calidris alpina*
Bonelli's Eagle	*Hieraaetus fasciatus*
Crested Serpent Eagle	*Spilornis cheela*
Eastern Steppe Eagle	*Aquila rapax nipalensis*
Greater Spotted Eagle	*Aquila clanga*
Imperial Eagle	*Aquila heliaca*
Lesser Spotted Eagle	*Aquila pomarina*
Pallas's Fishing Eagle	*Haliaetus leucoryphus*
Short-toed Eagle	*Circaetus gallicus*
Tawny Eagle	*Aquila rapax vindhiana*
Whitetailed Eagle	*Haliaeetus albicilla*
Cattle Egret	*Bubulcus ibis*
Large Egret	*Ardea alba*
Little Egret	*Egretta garzetta*
Smaller Egret	*Egretta intermedia*
Laggar Falcon	*Falco biarmicus jugger*
Lanner Falcon	*Falco biarmicus cherrug*
Peregrine Falcon	*Falco peregrinus japonensis*
Ashycrowned Finch-Lark	*Eremopterix grisea*
Desert Finch-Lark	*Ammomanes deserti*
Rufoustailed Finch-Lark	*Ammomanes phoenicurus*
Greater Flamingo	*Phoenicopterus roseus*
Thickbilled Flowerpecker	*Dicaeum agile*
Tickell's Flowerpecker	*Dicaeum erythrorhynchos*
Greyheaded Flycatcher	*Culicicapa ceylonensis*
Paradise Flycatcher	*Terpsiphone paradisi*
Redbreasted Flycatcher	*Muscicapa parva*
Rufoustailed Flycatcher	*Muscicapa ruficauda*
Tickell's Blue Flycatcher	*Muscicapa tickelliae*

Common name	Scientific name
Whitebrowed Blue Flycatcher	*Muscicapa superciliaris*
Whitebrowed Fantail Flycatcher	*Rhipidura aureola*
Gadwall	*Anas strepera*
Blacktailed Godwit	*Limosa limosa*
Barheaded Goose	*Anser indicus*
Greylag Goose	*Anser anser*
Whitefronted Goose	*Anser albifrons*
Goshawk	*Accipiter gentiles*
Great Crested Grebe	*Podiceps cristatus*
Little Grebe	*Tachybaptus ruficollis*
Greenshank	*Tringa nebularia*
Blackheaded Gull	*Larus ridibundus*
Brownheaded Gull	*Larus brunnicephalus*
Great blackheaded Gull	*Larus ichthyaetus*
Herring Gull	*Larus argentatus*
Marsh Harrier	*Circus aeruginosus*
Pale Harrier	*Circus macrourus*
Common Hawk Cuckoo	*Cuculus varius*
Booted Hawk-eagle	*Hieraaetus pennatus*
Grey Heron	*Ardea cinerea*
Little Green Heron	*Ardeola striatus*
Night Heron	*Nycticorax nycticorax*
Pond Heron	*Ardeola grayii*
Purple Heron	*Ardea purpurea*
Oriental Hobby	*Falco severus*
Hoopoe	*Upupa epops*
Grey Hornbill	*Tockus birostris*
Black Ibis	*Pseudibis papillosa*
Glossy Ibis	*Plegadis falcinellus*
White Ibis	*Threskiornis aethiopica*
Common Iora	*Aegithina tiphia*
Marshall's Iora	*Aegithina nigolutea*

Common name	Scientific name
Bronzewinged Jacana	*Metopidius indicus*
Pheasant-tailed Jacana	*Hydrophasianus chirurgus*
Kestrel	*Falco tinnunculus*
Common Kingfisher	*Alcedo atthis*
Lesser Pied Kingfisher	*Ceryle rudis*
Storkbilled Kingfisher	*Pelargopsis capensis*
Whitebreasted Kingfisher	*Halcyon smyrnensis*
Blackwinged Kite	*Elanus caeruleus*
Brahminy Kite	*Haliastur indus*
Pariah Kite	*Milvus migrans govinda*
Knot	*Calidris canutus*
Koel	*Eudynamys scolopacea*
Lapwing	*Vanellus vanellus*
Redwattled Lapwing	*Vanellus indicus*
Spurwinged Lapwing	*Vanellus spinosus*
Whitetailed Lapwing	*Vanellus leucurus*
Yellowwattled Lapwing	*Vanellus malabaricus*
Crested Lark	*Galerida cristata*
Redwinged Bush Lark	*Mirafra erythroptera*
Short-toed Lark	*Calandrella cinerea*
Singing Bush Lark	*Mirafra javanica*
Mallard	*Anas platyrhynchos*
Collared Sand Martin	*Riparia riparia*
Dusky Crag Martin	*Hirundo concolor*
Plain Sand Martin	*Riparia paludicola*
Scarlet Minivet	*Pericrocotus flammeus*
Small Minivet	*Pericrotus cinnamomeus*
Whitebellied Minivet	*Pericrocotus erythrroyygius*
Moorhen	*Gallinula chloropus*
Purple Moorhen	*Porphyrio porphyrio*
Blackheaded Munia	*Lonchura Malacca*
Red Munia	*Estrilda amandava*

Common name	Scientific name
Spotted Munia	*Lonchura punctulata*
Whitebacked Munia	*Lonchura striata*
Whitethroated Munia	*Lonchura malabarica*
Bank Myna	*Acridotheres ginginianus*
Brahminy Myna	*Sturnus pagodarum*
Common Myna	*Acridotheres tristis*
Greyheaded Myna	*Sturnus malabaricus*
Pied Myna	*Sturnus contra*
Common Indian Nightjar	*Caprimulgus asiaticus*
Franklin's Nightjar	*Caprimulgus affinis*
Indian Jungle Nightjar	*Caprimulgus indicus*
Syke's Nightjar	*Caprimulgus mahrettensis*
Chestnutbellied Nuthatch	*Sitta castanea*
Blackheaded Oriole	*Oriolus xanthornus*
Golden Oriole	*Oriolus oriolus*
Osprey	*Pandion haliaetus*
Scops Owl	*Otus scops*
Barn Owl	*Tyto alba*
Brown Fish Owl	*Bubo zeylonensis*
Collared Scops Owl	*Otus bakkamoena*
Dusky Horned Owl	*Bubo coromandus*
Great Horned Owl	*Bubo bubo*
Mottled Wood Owl	*Strix ocellata*
Shorteared Owl	*Asio flammeus*
Spotted Owlet	*Athene brama*
Alexandrine Parakeet	*Psittacula eupataria*
Blossomheaded Parakeet	*Psittacula cyanocephala*
Roseringed Parakeet	*Psittacula krameri*
Black Partridge	*Francolinus francolinus*
Grey Partridge	*Francolinus pondicerianus*
Rosy Pastor	*Sturnus roseus*
Common Peafowl	*Pavo cristatus*

Common name	Scientific name
Dalmatian Pelican	*Pelecanus philippensis crispus*
Spotbilled Pelican	*Pelecanus philippensis philipensis*
White Pelican	*Pelecanus onocrotalus*
Rednecked Phalarope	*Phalaropus lobatus*
Blue Rock Pigeon	*Columba livia*
Eastern Stock Pigeon	*Columba eversmanni*
Yellowlegged Green Pigeon	*Treron phoenicoptera*
Pintail	*Anas acuta*
Indian Tree Pipit	*Anthus hodgsoni*
Paddyfield Pipit	*Anthus novaeseelandiae*
Paddyfield Pipit	*Anthus novaeseelandiae richardi*
Tawny Pipit	*Anthus campestris*
Tree Pipit	*Anthus trivialis*
Vinaceousbreasted Pipit	*Anthus roseatus*
Water Pipit	*Anthus spinoletta*
Indian Pitta	*Pitta brachyura*
Eastern Golden Plover	*Pluvialis dominica*
Grey Plover	*Pluvialis squatarola*
Kentish Plover	*Charadrius alexandrinus*
Lesser Sand Plover	*Charadrius mongolus*
Little Ringed Plover	*Charadrius dubius*
Ringed Plover	*Charadrius hiaticula*
Baer's Pochard	*Aythya baeri*
Common Pochard	*Aythya ferina*
Redcrested Pochard	*Netta rufina*
White-eyed Pochard	*Aythya nyroca*
Collard Pratincole	*Glareola prantincola*
Small Indian Pratincole	*Glareola lactea*
Bluebreasted Quail	*Coturnix chinensis*
Common Quail	*Coturnix coturnix*
Common Bustard-quail	*Turnix suscitator*
Jungle Bush Quail	*Perdicula asiatica*

Common name	Scientific name
Little Bustard-quail	*Turnix sylvatica*
Rain Quail	*Coturnix coromandelica*
Water Rail	*Rallus aquaticus*
Common Redshank	*Tringa totanus*
Spotted Redshank	*Tringa erythropus*
Black Redstart	*Phoenicurus ochruros*
Indian Robin	*Saxicoloides fulicata*
Magpie Robin	*Copsychus saularis*
European Roller	*Coracias garralus*
Indian Roller	*Coracias benghalensis*
Common Rosefinch	*Carpodacus erythrinus*
Rubythroat	*Erithacus calliope*
Ruff and Reeve	*Philomachus pugnax*
Imperial Sandgrouse	*Pterocles orientalis*
Indian Sandgrouse	*Pterocles exustus*
Painted Sandgrouse	*Petrocles indicus indicus*
Broadbilled Sandpiper	*Limicola falcinellus*
Common Sandpiper	*Tringa hypoleucos*
Curlew Sandpiper	*Calidris testacea*
Green Sandpiper	*Tringa ochropus*
Terek Sandpiper	*Tringa terek*
Wood Sandpiper	*Tringa glareola*
Common Shelduck	*Tadorna tadorna*
Shikra	*Accipiter badius*
Shoveller	*Anas clypeata*
Baybacked Shrike	*Lanius vittatus*
Brown Shrike	*Lanius cristatus*
Grey Shrike	*Lanius excubitor*
Rufousbacked Shrike	*Lanius schach*
Eastern Skylark	*Alauda gulgula*
Jack Snipe	*Gallinago minima*
Fantail Snipe	*Gallinago gallinago*

Common name	Scientific name
Painted Snipe	*Rostratula benghalensis*
Pintail Snipe	*Gallinago stenura*
House Sparrow	*Passer domesticus*
Spanish Sparrow	*Passer hispaniolensis*
Tree Sparrow	*Passer montanus*
Yellowthroated Sparrow	*Petronia xanthyocollis*
Sparrow-hawk	*Accipter nisus nososimilis*
Besra Sparrow-hawk	*Accipiter virgatus*
Spoonbill	*Platalea leucorodia*
Painted Spurfowl	*Galloperdix lunulata*
Red Spurfowl	*Galloperdix spadicea*
Starling	*Sturnus vulgaris*
Blackwinged Stilt	*Himantopus himantopus*
Little Stint	*Calidris minuta*
Temminck's Stint	*Calidris temminckii*
Adjutant Stork	*Leptoptilos dubius*
Lesser Adjutant Stork	*Leptoptilos javanicus*
Black Stork	*Ciconia nigra*
Blacknecked Stork	*Ephippiorhynchus asiaticus*
Openbill Stork	*Anastomus oscitans*
Painted Stork	*Mycteria leucocephala*
White Stork	*Ciconia ciconia*
Whitenecked Stork	*Ciconia episcopus*
Purple Sunbird	*Nectarinia asiatica*
Swallow	*Hirundo rustica*
Indian Cliff Swallow	*Hirundo fluvicola*
Redrumped Swallow	*Hirundo daurica*
Wiretailed Swallow	*Hirundo smithii*
House Swift	*Apus affinis*
Alpine Swift	*Apus melba*
Palm Swift	*Cypsiurus parvus*
Tailor Bird	*Orthotomus sutorius*

Common name	Scientific name
Common Teal	*Anas crecca*
Cotton Teal	*Nettapus coromandelianus*
Lesser Whistling Teal	*Dendrocygna javanica*
Marbled Teal	*Marmaronetta angustirostris*
Falcated Teal	*Anas falcata*
Garganey Teal	*Anas querquedula*
Black Tern	*Chilidonias niger*
Blackbellied Tern	*Sterna acuticauda*
Gullbilled Tern	*Gelochelidon nilotica*
Indian River Tern	*Sterna aurantia*
Little Tern	*Sterna albifrons*
Whiskered Tern	*Chlidonias hybrida*
Blue Rock Thrush	*Monticola solitarius*
Orangeheaded Ground Thrush	*Zoothera citrina*
Tickell's Thrush	*Turdus unicolor*
Grey Tit	*Parus major*
Indian Tree Pie	*Dendrocitta vagabunda*
Turnstone	*Arenaria interpres*
Black Vulture	*Sarcogyps calvus*
Egyptian Vulture	*Neophron pernopterus*
Griffon Vulture	*Gyps fulvus*
Longbilled Vulture	*Gyps indicus*
Whitebacked Vulture	*Gyps bengalensis*
Grey Wagtail	*Motacilla cinerea*
Large Pied Wagtail	*Motacilla maderaspatensis*
White Wagtail	*Motacilla alba*
Yellow Wagtail	*Motacilla flava melanogrisea*
Yellowheaded Wagtail	*Motacilla citreola*
Booted Warbler	*Hippolais caligata*
Cetti's Warbler	*Cettia cetti*
Desert Warbler	*Sylvia nana*
Indian Great Reed Warbler	*Acrocephalus stentoreus*

Common name	Scientific name
Moustached Sedge Warbler	*Acrocephalus melanopogon*
Orphean Warbler	*Sylvia hortensis*
Paddyfield Warbler	*Acrocephalus agricola*
Streaked Fantail Warbler	*Cisticola juncidis*
Streaked Grasshopper Warbler	*Locustella lanceolata*
Thickbilled Warbler	*Acrocephalus aedon*
Brook's Leaf Warbler	*Phylloscopus subviridis*
Brown Leaf Warbler	*Phylloscopus collybita*
Dusky Leaf Warbler	*Phylloscopous fuscatus*
Greenish Leaf Warbler	*Phylloscopus trochiloides*
Largecrowned Leaf Warbler	*Phylloscopus occipitalis*
Olivaceous Leaf Warbler	*Phylloscopus griseolus*
Tickell's Leaf Warbler	*Phylloscopus affinis*
Tytler's Leaf Warbler	*Phylloscopus tytleri*
Yellowbrowed Leaf Warbler	*Phylloscopus inornatus*
Ashy Wren Warbler	*Prinia socialis stewarti*
Ashy Grey Wren Warbler	*Prinia hodgsonii*
Jungle Wren Warbler	*Prinia sylvatica*
Plain Wren Warbler	*Prinia subflava*
Rufousfronted Wren Warbler	*Prinia buchanani*
Watercock	*Gallicrex cinerea*
Whitebreasted Waterhen	*Amaurornis phoenicurus*
Baya Weaver	*Ploceus philippinus*
Blackthroated Weaver	*Ploceus benghalensis*
Streaked Weaver	*Ploceus manyar*
Desert Wheatear	*Oenanthe deserti*
Whitethroat	*Sylvia communis*
Lesser Whitethroat	*Sylvia curruca*
Lesser Whitethroat	*Sylvia curruca althaea*
White-eye	*Zosterops palpebrosa*
Wigeon	*Anas penelope*
Lesser Goldenbacked Woodpecker	*Dinopium benghalense*

Common name	Scientific name
Pigmy Woodpecker	*Piciodes nanus*
Yellowfronted Pied Woodpecker	*Piciodes mahrattensis*
Common Woodshrike	*Tephrodornis pondicerianus*
Wryneck	*Jynx torquilla*

Note: Bird names are consistent with usage in Ali and Ripley, 1998.

Tigers

While most tourists entering Sariska are in pursuit of that Holy Grail—the sighting of a tiger—I have kept up my interest in other, less glamorous sights. The sight of the first hill burnished with the rust leaves of 'dhok', as you cross over the hill into the Kalighati valley, the leaf-fringed avenue of 'dhok' that greets the visitor at the old gate leading to Kankwari, the sound of the Algual rill, overgrown on both sides with old trees of 'guler' and 'pilkhan', the sight of an explosion of Bluebreasted Quail from nearly below the tyres of the Gypsy, the deep pools of the Siliberi Nala flowing down from Pandupol, with Pallas' Fishing Eagles watching for prey from nearby evergreen trees, the feeding on hand of tree pies at Kalighati *chauki*—all these and more have been the joys of numerous visits to Sariska.

However, near-misses with big cats still make for better copy in Delhi. Never mind that we saw six porcupine in the course of an early evening drive near Umri. Or that we saw the reclusive Indian Pitta at Taraunda hide late in the evening. If every second tourist Gypsy entering Sariska left with magnificent cat sightings, even my wife was once moved to ask why it was that we never saw a tiger?

And so our luck with the predator turned. Late in the evening four winters past, we heard the alarm calls near the check-dam at Slopka, and following the sounds, we saw the tiger in silhouette climb up the far hill towards Jahaj. The profile was clear, the length of tail characteristic, but it wasn't enough. We had to see one in the clear light of day.

Finally, in the hot month of April the next year, my wife and I were privileged to have a close sighting of a tiger just beyond Kalighati. In the late morning, as we were returning past Bhaironghati from a car drive to Pandupol, we stopped near the salt lick short of Kalighati *chauki*. We saw the 'langurs' climb up the trees on the hillside. They soon started calling. Then it was the turn of a 'sambar' concealed in the grass. The loud 'dhank' was unmistakable. A predator was moving nearby. We drove down the crest of the hill in case we should miss the animal. Before long, we heard the loud and impressive calls of a tiger, and then we saw him cross the road behind us, with no care or concern for our presence. Perhaps it was late in the morning; there was little chance of a meal, and he was in a hurry to get to the waterhole behind the hill. We were grateful for the unimpeded view.

Sariska without tigers would be hard to imagine. The history of the Park's protection has revolved around the organized *shikar* and, later, the protection of its tigers. Most visitors have been drawn to Sariska by the prospect of relatively easy tiger sightings. Over time, Sariska has become synonymous with tiger. Until 2004, that is.

Tigers haven't been seen by forest officials since June of 2004, while the last tourist claims to have seen the tiger in November. The entire tiger population couldn't have migrated away from the one central protected area with game and Forest Department invigilation. The suspicion of poaching is strong, pending the findings of the studies underway. Poaching can explain the absence of tigers, it cannot explain why there were so few in the first place . . . the Park must reclaim the 75 percent of its habitat which has been degraded by grazing and lopping. Village rights must be settled, some villages generously rehabilitated outside the Park, and the Park subsequently notified. The Prime Minister has rightly called this latest tiger crisis 'the biggest crisis in the management of our wildlife' since the launch of Project Tiger. With the all public attention this crisis has generated, the initiative to put conservation efforts at Sariska on a stronger footing must not be lost.

1. Typical Sariska grassland with 'ber' trees

2. Gateway to Kankwari with canopy of 'dhok' trees

3. Evergreen forests fed by the Algual spring

4. Approaching Kalighati *chauki*

5. Kankwari fort in profile, showing fortified approach

6. Temple ruins at Neelkanth

7. The eastern park boundary

8. Looking towards Umri plateau from Pandupol

9. Pandupol rock bridge

10. Kankwari plateau framed by Rajput-style cusped arch

11. Neelkanth Mahadev

12. Siliberi stream-bed with 'khajur' trees

13. Kankwari fort with receding forest in the background

14. Siliberi *nallah* near Pandupol with 'khajur' trees

15. White-eyed Buzzard-eagle

16. Shikra

17. Barheaded Geese at Tehla

18. Whitebreasted Kingfisher

19. Indian Nightjar

20. Blue Jay or Indian Roller

21. A pair of Coucals or Crow Pheasants

22. Painted Spurfowl

23. Yellowlegged Green Pigeon

24. Painted Sandgrouse

25. Anisha feeding tree pies

26. 'Sambhar' doe with tree pie

27. 'Nilgai' male

28. Palm Civet or Toddy Cat

29. Sounder of wild boar

30. 'Langur' in portrait

31. 'Cheetal' stag

32. 'Sambhar' stag

2

Critical Issues in Park Management

Land Settlement

The lack of consistent management priorities has blunted some of the benefits which resulted from the inclusion of Sariska under Project Tiger in 1978-79. In the absence of priorities for long-term management, even the protection of the land area has been neglected. With land settlement incomplete to this day, large areas of the park have been encroached upon for agriculture and mining. Encroachment continues all the time, besides the temple complex at Neelkanth, near Bhartrihari, or by the shores of Siliserh Lake, what to speak of the insular and adjoining villages.

The major controversy at Sariska through the years has been whether or not water should be provided to animals in the summer. The critical issues of settlement of boundaries, resettlement of insular villages, management of tourist traffic, and degradation of the buffer have not been meaningfully addressed. No doubt these are very difficult problems for the forest administration alone to deal with;

in the absence of political will at the district and state levels they are almost intractable. This critique laments the position of concerned and highly motivated forest officials; there is so much beyond their domain.

The boundaries of the sanctuary and the proposed national park, as well as the reserved and protected forests in the area, have not yet been settled. In various gazettes, these boundaries are indicated by straight lines between outlying villages. With the gradual incursion of the villages into forest land, these lines are no longer meaningful. The forest is besieged from all corners today. The most fertile valley of Panidhal has been cultivated for the last thirty years, and forest and revenue lands of the adjacent villages have not been settled by a procedure called 'Amal darmat.' As a result, local revenue officials have actually distributed forest land for resettlement. Some 41 blocks of the sanctuary have been cleared for allotment by revenue authorities. All this has had deleterious impacts on park management. Mining permits were given because the land mined was 'appropriated' as revenue land. The park administration put out a No Objection Certificate (NOC) for these mines a few years ago and 288 open-cast mines were allowed to operate in 'Core Area Three' of Sariska Sanctuary till the Supreme Court judgement of 1997 stopped much of the mining. It is left to conjecture what the erstwhile administration was thinking about when the NOC was given. Buffer zones have been made non-existent with ongoing encroachment and progressive degradation owing to grazing and firewood collection. Some of the sanctuary forests are still being worked for timber by the Alwar DFO.

Successive Field Directors have grappled with the issues of boundaries which bedevil the development of Sariska as a conservation unit. One of the previous Director's, sitting at his desk, moaned the fact that he did not even know if his office in Sariska was in 'Roondh' forest/reserved forest/ Sanctuary/the proposed national park. *Roondh* category is a relic of the Alwar administration of the pre-independence days. To this day there hasn't been a settlement on ground according to these categories. The park forests have not even been accorded Reserved Forest status under the Rajasthan Forest Act, 1953, what to speak of final notification of national park status upon the eventual conclusion of the process of evaluating rights (begun in 1975!).

While offenders are fully cognizant of the slow process of land classification and their rights as settlers in a democratic state (they will at least be compensated if eviction ever comes to pass, and this will become well-nigh impossible if the ill-conceived Tribal Rights Bill is soon passed in its current from), the forest department is completely immobilized by lack of information on notification. A few years ago, the relocation of Umri village was stopped. The plan for resettlement had been approved by the Government of India and accepted by the villagers. Finances for this resettlement have been deposited in Alwar. The scheme was suspended after wells had been dug in an area some 20 km away from the village. All because no government official in New Delhi wants to sign away forest land, never mind the compromised situation on the ground. It turned out that the land where these people were being moved was actually forest land, for which the notification was still pending after thirty years. Notification has apparently been consistently ignored by successive park administrations at Sariska. While this was not a problem thirty years ago when the process should have started, it is one of the most important problems threatening the existence of this forest area today.

Poaching

In the early 90s some 19 tigers were killed in one year at Sariska. The actual number must have been higher. It was found that there was a regular group of poachers—local Baorias—who operated on small commissions from agents of a large enterprise in Delhi's Sadar Bazaar. The lack of the right to investigate has hindered prosecution in case of tiger killings in the past. Three years ago a tiger's carcass was reported as dead livestock and thrown into a lake. And now, the entire tiger population is missing!

Related to the issue of poaching is the whole issue of research and monitoring of animal population—both of which are somewhat neglected. Previous censuses conducted at Sariska counted over 70 pythons and twice the number of Ratels, and classified them by sex—all in one night. It is gratifying to note, though, that the drivers of tourist Gypsies have volunteered to help with recent censuses. An independent research programme could be initiated at Sariska to highlight the state of the park's ecological health and suggest long-term remedial measures. The next census will no doubt settle the mystery of the missing tigers of 2004-2005. But, surely this should have been known at least six months earlier.

Tourism and Traffic

Apart from the draw of wildlife, Sariska harbours many pilgrimage sites and old temples such as Pandupol, Talvriksh, Rajoregarh, Neelkanth and Bhartrihari. These sites attract legion visitors year-round. In August/September, a fair is held in the park, drawing 200,000 pilgrims in 1000 vehicles! Over 400 vehicles are given free entry twice a week (Tuesdays and Saturdays) to drive to Pandupol via Kalighati, the only habitation-free stretch of forest in the park. There are now 8 buses transiting through the park daily. Commercial vehicles have recently started carrying milk from Kankwari and Keraska villages to the towns outside. All this continues throughout the year, with no rest for the monsoon—making for a quantum of traffic few other parks in India have to contend with.

To add to the pilgrim traffic, over a dozen *babas* have set up *ashrams* near permanent water sources such as Udainath. Good forest and permanent water sources are alienated from wildlife through the disturbance created by these anti-forest godmen and their acolytes. One enterprising *baba* was caught trading in 'cheetal' skins.

Fortunately, there is now a set of rules in place—to caution wildlife tourists about blaring their horns, playing loud music, and straying off permitted roads in the park. An effort at conservation education is a welcome addition, so tourists leave the park wiser than when they entered. Even wildlife tourism traffic has grown to such proportions that it needs to be spread over a larger area of the park, possibly even through Core Area One. There is little joy for anyone in a long line of Gypsies waiting to enter the park and travel on the same beaten track!

Buffer Zone Development

One of biggest challenges to park management at Sariska (made more difficult, no doubt, by the non-completion of notification of boundaries) has been the management of the buffer, especially considering the high pressure from the peripheral population. The development of a buffer zone is one of the priorities of Project Tiger, which has been in operation in Sariska for 20 years. While successive administrators have been successful in managing the tiger population (sometimes on file) and the related prey population (at least around the Pandupol road), buffer zone development has been a total non-starter. The buffer is actually non-existent. As one travels on the Alwar-Jaipur road, it is shocking to see the degraded forests along the border of the park. Grazing and lopping of *dhok* continues unabated in these peripheral areas which are being converted to wastelands in the absence of any management intervention.

The conflict between people and the park is not restricted to the villages in the park. Wild animals from Sariska cause considerable damage to crops and prey on the livestock of surrounding villages as well. Crop and livestock depredation was found to affect over half of the households in villages adjacent to Sariska (Sekhar, 1998). The 'nilgai' and the wild boar are responsible for nearly half of all the damage to crops, and tiger and leopard are the main livestock predators. Even though two-thirds of the villagers in the areas around

Sariska spend considerable time and expense guarding crops and protecting livestock, local people were found to have a positive attitude towards the park. This stems from strongly-held cultural attitudes to wild animals, as well as tangible benefits obtained from the park including fodder and fuel-wood. This healthy tolerance offers hope that buffer zone development in the mutual interest of the park and the outlying villages can be made to work. If local people were preferred for forestry works and even as forest guards, building support for the park would be made much easier. During drought years, the park could permit grass removal from the buffer in a controlled manner.

Access and Control

It is not clear that the park authorities are winning the battle to maintain custodial control over non-central areas of the park. There is evidence of grazing almost upto Kalighati. Forest roads have not been maintained to the Panidhal Core, a splendid area of rich forest land, which is no longer connected to the Central Core. In fact, the access road has itself been diverted by villagers who have encroached on forest land. *Guadas* or cattle camps, which were once evicted, have returned to Panidhal, with permanent construction this time. The lack of invigilation which results from not having well-maintained forest roads results in encroachment, grazing, and possibly, poaching. The road to the eastern boundary from the main park entrance is no longer in operation. This was an important road for observations on the eastern side. The forest approach to Keraska via the Algual spring, which is excellent habitat for carnivores, has simply vanished.

The forest *chauki* at Algual is no longer manned, and it is no wonder that villagers are now coming down to Algual spring to wash their clothes. Kankwari and its adjoining villages are spreading a swathe of grazing and lopping-induced devastation in concentric circles around the plateau to include wildlife-rich habitats like Mala, even as livestock herds multiply and there is no invigilation and not even a manned *chauki* on the plateau. Why is this situation coming to a pass, when perfectly reasonable forest tracks and a *chauki* had been established previously? This lack of invigilation might well explain the persistent rumours of poaching of large mammals. The situation at Kankwari has worsened only in the last 10 years as invigilation has ceased and political activism spurred by controversial NGOs has increased.

The maintenance of forest roads serves another purpose—to disperse the overdose of tourist traffic within Sariska. The movement of tourists and guides on these lesser-travelled roads would help improve invigilation of non-central areas and provide visitors with a more varied itinerary than simply the central drive to Pandupol. Tourism can be channeled to good use in this manner. The construction of road access to Pandupol via Siliberi and Umri would reduce traffic on the central axis and help its conservation immeasurably, besides improving invigilation by the southern entrance. Some efforts have been made in the central area with access to the Kundli anicut and its cane brakes and splendid 'dhok' forest. Similarly, the new road to Pandupol via the hilltop above Slopka opens up a new area and evidences fine 'salai', 'tendu', and 'dhawa' forest. The Doraka track shows up the fine forests of Bamboo, 'dhok' and 'dhawa' trees north of the Jahaj area.

Watch-towers which were used for game-watching at Sariska, such as at Taraunda, are now in disrepair and no longer used by visitors. This is a sorry state of affairs and bodes ill for efforts against poaching. Again, the maintenance of watch-towers would provide alternatives to that over-travelled Pandupol drive, as well as improve invigilation. Forest *chaukis* at the peripheries are also not being maintained or manned. Algual, Kankwari, and Panidhal *chaukis* have been abandoned.

Highway Relocation

Multi-crore funds (Rs. 4.2 crore) have been provided for relocation of the Alwar-Thana Ghazi State Highway which runs through the park for 30 km. This is a laudable objective, given the accidents to animals on the road (a tigress was killed near the Sariska Palace Hotel on the 4th of June 1997). Routing the truck traffic (1000 trucks daily) via Narayanpur and Ghata-Bandhrole is a sensible option, and this effort must be sustained.

Meanwhile, the central Alwar-Jaipur road has been provided additional speed traps at sensitive locations and *pulias* (culverts) for facilitating the animal crossings. Improved management of traffic on this road can help reclaim the rich roadside forests (such as those near Bandipul where a tigress has raised two cubs two years ago) for both wildlife and tourism purposes. Finally, the Sariska-Tehla road should be closed for commercial traffic and an alternative provided outside the park.

Park Expansion

Much is made of the possibilities for park expansion. This is a pipe-dream while many areas of Sariska itself are not under the watch and ward of the park authorities. So much more is needed to control what forest exists in Core Areas One and Three before new areas are brought under park management. Park expansion is no doubt a laudable idea, but the management should find ways to first consolidate gains made, and then work on re-integrating the three Core Areas which are fragmenting through encroachment. Panidhal has to be brought under active park management, and road access established for invigilation and tourism before anything else is done on the park expansion front. This is a fine forest area, with even more potential for wildlife than the central vista to Pandupol, and it is completely neglected. Eventual expansion could also include the Alwar forests in the north-east, including Bala Qila fort and its unparalleled *Anogeissus* forests; other areas include Siliserh-Sirawas and areas in the direction of Digota-Bhangarh (Jaipur West Division) to eventually provide the 35 km linkage to the Jamwa-Ramgarh Sanctuary (itself covering an area of 300 sq km), and its Shakun Odhi. In the meantime, a core area, free of human disturbance, could be established right away at Jamwa-Ramgarh itself.

3

Challenges of Village Resettlement

Ecological Crisis

The major management and ecological challenge at Sariska is that of 16 village settlements inside the forest, harbouring around 5000 people and 30,000 head of cattle. The pressure from the outside is even greater—a human population of 250,000 and a cattle population of 100,000 was estimated in 1989 (Mathur, 1991). Another report mentions a human population of 108,000 regularly collecting fuelwood, fodder, and timber from the park (Sekhar, 1998). The villages around the park report an annual human population growth rate of 1.5 percent. The livestock density in the district in nearly twice that of the average for Rajasthan. In the last two decades, the buffalo population has grown 70 percent, while the goat population has grown 40 percent. Nearly 55 percent of the livestock are dependent on the park for grazing, competing daily with wildlife for grass and water, besides spreading disease to the wild ungulates. Given these numbers, it is not a surprise to read that 74 percent of the villages surveyed around Sariska also report crop damage by wild animals as a problem (Sekhar, 1988). It is these figures that suggest a bleak picture of the future of Sariska, and, indeed for the natural ecology of the Aravallis.

The Revenue villages inside the park include Madhogarh, Indhok, Nangalheri, Duhar Mala, Mithrawat, Kaniyawas, Raika Mala, Garh, Rajore, Devri, Dabli, Kushalgarh, Kala-chara, Keraska, Kundalka, and Bairawas. Only Karnakabas has been resettled to date. Of these settlements, Devri, Dabli, and Keraska are located in the Core Area of the park. In addition, there are numerous temporary *guadas* which have become more-or-less permanent, including Kankwari, Umri, Haripura, Lilonda, and Sukola. Only two *guadas*—Siliberi and Ganka—have been resettled. The national park is today an island of wilderness in a densely cultivated, fragmenting, and populated landscape.

A study conducted by the Wildlife Institute of India found that 60 percent of the park was affected by the grazing pressure emanating from these villagers. An earlier study in Ranthambhor, another park in the Aravallis in Rajasthan, revealed that nearly 85 per cent of the Core Area was affected by grazing and collection of firewood (Berkmuller, 1988). Another study by the Wildlife Institute of India (Mathur, 1991) has concluded that 'sambar' and 'cheetal' numbers decline in habitats where livestock grazing is intense. 'Sambar' competes with goats for browse material, and with cattle for water, which is needed for wallowing and drinking. 'Cheetal' is a grazer and so competes with cattle for feed and water. 'Nilgai' is the least disturbed by cattle since browse material comprises 70 percent of its diet, and the animal needs water less frequently. The WII study found that construction of a rubble wall around Haripura was found to be beneficial for the wild ungulates, by leading to an increase in the grass forage volume in the nearby forest.

Not only the ungulates, a later study found that even the 'langur' population density was significantly higher in undisturbed areas (Ross and Srivastava, 1994). This stands to reason, since there may not be enough food to support the 'langur' population in disturbed areas with low tree density. Tree density, tree cover, and the number of tree species are lower in disturbed areas, suggesting the quantity and variety of food is reduced in these areas at Sariska. Apparently, nearly 10 percent of the 'langur' population at Ranthambhor is preyed on by tiger annually (reported in Ross and Srivastava, 1994). Therefore, greater disturbance to the 'langurs' also directly lowers the tiger's prey base.

Almost the entire ungulate population of Sariska (approx. 3000 head of cheetal, 5000 sambhar, and 4500 nilgai) is today concentrated in only 20 percent of the park area which is free of grazing by insular village livestock—the stretch from Taraunda to Pandupol. Removal of insular villages would disperse the animals to disturbed areas that are out of bounds today. Further, the presence of weeds such as 'adusa' (*Adhatoda vesica*), 'panwar' (*Cassia tora*), 'vilayti babul' (*Prosopis juliflora*), and 'lantana' (*Lantana camara*), is entirely a result of overgrazing by village cattle, and has affected nearly 64 sq km of the productive core area of the park across Sariska, Tehla, Akbarpur and Talvriksh ranges.

Sociological Challenge

The difference between undisturbed vegetation, and vegetation degraded because of overgrazing, is stark and pervasive at Sariska. Most of the settlement rights and concessions were granted over a hundred years ago. In the meantime, India's forest cover has shrunk dramatically—that of the northern Aravallis almost to nothing. Deforestation is in part aggravated by urban demand for fuelwood and milk. Local people who live in the forest villages and cut trees become law-breakers. In poverty, their population continues to increase (as does that of their livestock). Consequently grazing, once very profitable, is now wrought with misery and poverty. These forest-dwelling people are denied all the changes brought about by development in the surrounding areas (health care, electricity, education) because they are trapped in the forest, in a cycle of poverty and ecological degradation.

The question of relocation of indigenous forest people and villagers who have rights and concessions in forest areas remains controversial in India, with only a few successful resettlement programmes. Villagers at Sariska naturally retain apprehensions about resettlement. One previous translocation programme at Sariska was a failure for the villagers, with outsiders and zamindars gleaning most of the benefits. This has frightened the remaining villagers from moving. Clearly, the resettlement of the village did help the park, and the area surrounding the old village of Karnakabas has recovered and now hosts a productive *jheel*. In the absence of better livelihoods for the displaced villagers, displacement from the park has become controversial and unpopular.

Given the prosperity of the villagers finally resettled near Ajaibgarh, a stronger case can now be made for resettlement. Especially when villagers themselves are now asking for change, provided such change gives them better facilities and a fair deal. Why the government is now taking an unprogressive view on resettlement is a complete about-face and mystery.

The views and apprehensions of villagers are understandable. Villagers in Sariska are not intentional culprits in overgrazing and collection of firewood from the park. They are caught in an increasingly unsustainable life-style and cannot break out of it on their own. They welcome the idea of government inputs but are wary of resettlement. Elders in general are hesitant because they view the forests as a great security against drought. Why should they suffer from the risk of schemes like the controversial resettlements of Keraska and Kundalka, in which villagers returned to Sariska on not obtaining the benefits of relocation? The park authorities, on the other hand, claim the villagers simply took the benefits and returned back to the park, spurred by local politicians and NGOs.

The Tarun Bharat Sangh (TBS), an NGO based in Bhikampura village, had earlier persuaded villagers to oppose resettlement. TBS has done a commendable job in providing education to villagers living in Sariska. TBS has also cooperated with park authorities in building check-dams (which have not worked, being incorrectly sited). The movement of milk trucks in the park has also been organized by them. While these have been useful exercises in building up TBS's support among the villagers, TBS has finally come around to supporting resettlement, leaving villagers even more confused. Eventually, the park authorities and villagers will have to build a direct working relationship based on trust and participation to deliver on just and fair resettlement programmes.

Chhal Singh Gujjar of Umri village in the interior of Sariska (which is slated to be one of the first to be resettled) reports that around 80 animals die from the annual drought in his *guada* alone. He would be happy to move if adequate land of at least five bighas is offered. The grasslands surrounding his village have been colonized by *Cassia tora* and *Adhatoda vesica*. 'Dhak' and 'salai' have stopped regenerating. His buffaloes spread outwards in ever-widening circles to look for fodder, even though they are often fined. Umri village has 26 families with 200 people, 600 buffaloes, 100 cows and 600 goats (Johnsingh, et al., 2001). The village is over 20 km away from medical and school facilities. Land has previously been identified for resettlement of Umri at Dabkan near Thana Ghazi, but the resettlement plans have been shelved sine die.

Keraska comprises two picturesque village settlements isolated on top of the Aravalli plateau on the eastern side of Sariska. As soon as one leaves the excellent mixed forest of the hillside to reach the plateau, one is treated to a swathe of habitat destruction around these villages. Clearly the villages are not living in some Utopian harmony with Nature, as some NGOs contend. Keraska villagers have constructed walls to prevent 'nilgai' and 'sambar' from raiding crops and drinking water from the lake. Within these walls, which do not correspond to the legal boundaries of these revenue villagers, there is absolutely no vegetation left. Dev Karan, an elder of Pehlagaon, regales us with the story of the block development officer (BDO) who told the villagers of Keraska that officially they did not exist. Naturally, Keraska villagers are not then provided any administrative facilities whatsoever. However, the BDO promised a school teacher who came to the village for a month. He soon returned alleging no one in Keraska was interested in education. These people have fertile lands and free firewood and grazing. They live an idyllic life, even though they are desperately poor and have no access to development. Yet even their population is rising and their impact on the habitat becoming progressively destructive.

In contrast, the villagers of Haripura, which is a village situated on a small hill near the Thana Ghazi entrance of the park, are alert and worldly wise. They are chary of the sanctuary administration whose staff often tie up their goats to ask for 'unreceipted fines.' They have understood the consequences of fully 'trusting' the government as their neighbours in Karnakabas did, and have no intention of moving if they can help it. Yet they bemoan their rising debts and increasing friction with the sanctuary authorities and realize that one day they may have to leave the forest.

From an ecological standpoint, it is essential that insular villages are resettled. Their livestock, which is the mainstay of their existence, cannot be sustainably supported in the forest remaining at Sariska. The question is whether the government's support for conservation extends to executing such attractive and humane rehabilitation schemes that resettlement becomes a compelling alternative for pastoralists and cultivators alike settled in forest lands at Sariska.

A total of Rs. 4.3 crore is currently being considered for the rehabilitation of the first four villages—Umri (beyond the central valley), Keraska (on the eastern plateau), Bhagani, and Kankwari (on the western plateau). The affected villagers are to be granted two acres of farmland per head to cultivate near Tehla. Enough vacillation and activism has taken place, and the lives of the Sariska forest villagers are not better for it. They are completely cut off, and would opt for a fair resettlement, were it not for the constant needling by ill-motivated NGOs/political activists. Growing swathes of barren land surround these villages, degraded by increasing livestock population. There can be no progress for Sariska without attending to this problem. This first resettlement programme must be designed with intensive input by the villagers themselves, and executed transparently under full public scrutiny. The credibility of this effort will determine the course of the remaining villages.

Conclusion

By focusing on the major management issues discussed—village resettlement, forest road construction and improved invigilation, repair of watch-towers, manning of forest *chaukis*, buffer zone development, and park consolidation—Sariska can achieve its potential as one of the finest wildlife areas in India.

The enhancement of conservation at Sariska would also support the long-term development of Alwar district. The long-term development benefits include enhanced water flow in summer, job opportunities provided by the park and wildlife tourism, provision of fodder from the buffer in lean periods, participatory and voluntary resettlement of neglected, insular villages, and, finally, eco-development projects focusing on fuel and livestock.

4

Wildlife Conservation in Contemporary India

As countries develop, environmental issues emerge at the forefront of public attention. Prosperity affords and builds public support for meaningful environmental management. This includes the conservation of wilderness areas. People and institutions in developed countries are now even examining environmental problems on a larger global scale (Cairncross, 1991; Colby 1990; Goodland, 1990; Gregersen, 1989; McNeely, 1990a; Rich, 1994).

In India, despite our early idealism, and the tradition of respect and love for nature and the wilderness, we are still struggling to protect our forest and wildlife wealth (Davidar, 1997; Dharamkumarsinhji, 1999; Guha, 2000; Karanth, 2001; Ranjitsinh, 1997; Saharia, 1982).

In the last 50 years, as we have failed to combat poverty, control population, and invest in our people, we have also lost most of the wilderness areas, the forests, the *khadars* and the 'scrub-lands' (now called wastelands), that an earlier generation grew up roaming and loving with a grand passion. There are very few great 'mahaseer' fish in the Himalayan streams now. The tiger—the symbol of the Indian forest—is decimated and could be heading for extinction unless we change our short-sighted, narrow-minded, election-oriented policies, inspite of the much-publicized Project Tiger. With the near-demise of the tiger, we have lost much of its prey and its *rahans* and habitat. The wild and forested lands of 'roar, trumpet and song' continue to recede and reel under 'democratic' social and human pressure, and virtually non-existent grassroots resource management and increasing field indifference. Forests have been settled under electoral pressure all across the wildlands of India. Poaching, timber theft, over-grazing, and imperfectly planned and uneconomic public sector projects, too numerous to mention, have undermined or destroyed much of the remaining climax forests, especially those outside the limited network of small national parks. We can neither present a successful Indian model of harmonious living with nature, nor a successful model of rapid, environmentally-sustainable economic and human resource development.

The imperatives of growth leading to increased environmental stress, and the urgency of saving threatened bio-diversity and its wilderness habitat through protection, have generated a tragic conflict between the competing demands of development and conservation, which has been amply described by scholars and practitioners in the field (Dang, 1991b; Goodland, 1989; Mishra, 1984; Saharia, 1984). In the meantime, there has also been a lot of research on how to reconcile this conflict between 'people and parks' (CSE,

1989; Dang, 1997; Hough, 1990; Kiss, 1990; Kothari, 1996; McNeely, 1989; McNeely, 1990b; Misra, 1984; Panwar, 1984; Panwar, 1985; Poole, 1989; Saharia, 1984; Viksat, 1991; Wells, 1990).

The conflicting interests of development and conservation in India will only intensify, with the continuing, unsustainable and unbalanced human and livestock population growth rates, and the associated aspirational pressures of our people and our successful, federal democratic polity (Dang and Dang, 1998). This over-regulated and under-governed country does not naturally lend itself to rational land-use or efficient natural resource planning. This is one reason why American and European models of conservation, and the emerging ecological slant in environmental thinking abroad, will not address India's contemporary socio-economic situation. Industrialized countries of the G-7 are realizing that they can afford to place a higher emphasis on environmental values and afford more 'development' and less 'growth.' By contrast, in India, we are still to see explosive growth—of human and livestock populations, of material consumption and standards of living, of roads, electricity generation, fertilizer, coal and fuel consumption, airports and ports, urban and industrial waste, and so on. This prognosis of continued environmental stress is a fact of India's development and cannot be ignored (the avalanche of commercial threats to protected areas has been listed in Kutty, 2001). There may be more or less efficient economic models for India to use. But any country with a billion people, over half of whom are illiterate, and a majority of whom have no access to water, sewage, and health care, what to speak of jobs and social security, cannot afford not to both grow rapidly and to develop.

It is with this perspective that this section discusses ideas which could help save what we have left of India's precious wilderness habitats. These ideas have not been part of official or NGO conservation thinking in the past, and deserve scrutiny because the incremental approach of failing policies and fudged censuses, while paying lip-service to environmental platitudes will amount to no more than a re-arrangement of the deck chairs of the Titanic! If some of these ideas sound audacious, the facts about the perilous state of India's wildlife today are audacious and alarming, as has recently been recognized in the censure of India by CITES.

Releasing stamps on birds, organizing international environmental conferences, then using rubber-stamp committees to clear bizarre river-linking projects and manifold coastal zone infringements, and dereserving vast amounts of forest land at election time, is no longer credible environmental practice from the Indian state and its ministries. The Ministry specifically charged with environmental management simply becomes a permitting agency to facilitate the collections of private tolls in the interest of the 'public good.' Even the fig-leaf of token environmentalism has been dropped in the recent Tribal Rights Bill which will erode all the conservation efforts of the last 50 years.

The emerging themes in wildlife conservation described below have resulted from non-official, in-depth study visits to key protected areas. They suggest how contemporary India, in the process of economic liberalization, increasingly directed to higher rates of economic growth, can better manage her natural patrimony. These tentative suggestions involve a greater participatory role for various elements of Indian society, and a law-abiding approach on the part of the state.

Size Matters

There is little ultimate conservation value in increasing or establishing centrally-sponsored budgets for small sanctuaries which can hardly be extended, let alone protected effectively, given the insurmountable pressures from the surrounding areas. There may be other local reasons for states to protect these small parks, but from an ecosystem point of view, a park like Kanha in M.P. with an area greater than 2000 sq. km. offers more durable conservation value to preserve animal and plant species. Anathema as a comparison between the conservation values offered by different parks may sound, we have to recognize the fact that most of India's wildlife and wilderness areas will just not make it past the next 20 years. Some prioritization and effective management of at least a few select areas is better than losing everything! As it is, a good number of protected areas in India like Karera, Sitamata, Bhindawas, Noradehi, and Hastinapur, only exist on paper, and have little or nothing by way of budgets, security, park infrastructure or research capabilities.

Kanha National Park is already connected by continuous forest to Achanakmar Sanctuary near Amarkantak, the source of the Narmada river. The forested Maikal hills are also connected to the park to allow for the dispersion of wildlife. The nearby Phen Sanctuary is in the process of being added to Kanha. The forests adjacent and connected to Kanha thus add up to an area of some 5000-10,000 sq. km. The area can be increased further if the entire Satpuda-Maikal corridor is accorded protected status. This is an unbroken stretch of forest from Melghat to Achanakmar, including Melghat, Pench, Kanha, Bhoramdeo and Achanakmar, spanning forests from Maharashtra to Chhattisgarh. It is only in such a large area that viable populations of large mammals like tigers, and a representation of much of peninsular India's flora and fauna can exist. Some dozen tigers in Ranthambhor or Sariska National Parks may not be viable 20 years hence (in fact poachers, elitist over-exposure, and failure to manage resource conflicts have already taken care of this problem). Only professional Forest and Wildlife Service cadres, preferably with idealistic enthusiasm and dedication to the job, can sufficiently harden the environmental management of parks like Eturnagram, Pakhal, Mundanthurai, Gir, Tadoba, and the large number of smaller protected areas away from the public eye.

Forest corridors need urgent protection around Kanha before development catches up, even as the grazing populations have started rising (with rising human population). Poaching has been greatly controlled in Kanha. But animals from Kanha are being regularly killed outside (in the Balaghat area) and there is a flourishing animal trade market in Baihar. If the tiger needs to be saved, a stronger effort is needed for greater Kanha than for all the small parks combined. For other reasons, and other animals, conservation efforts are needed at the small parks, too. But these should be supplemental to creating a few key park complexes, which are large, well managed, centrally-funded, and politically inviolate.

Another park in Madhya Pradesh, Bandhavagarh National Park, has now been extended to include Pan Patha Sanctuary. Like Kanha, Bandhavagarh is also surrounded by degraded buffer forests. Bandhavagarh can easily be extended to a size of more than 2000 sq km by including the Vindhyan hills and extending the park boundary all the way to the Johilla river. Any extension will involve the removal of several insular villages. Given that the park authorities have not been able to remove six villages in the current park area for more than ten years, much more will have to be done to design a successful rehabilitation scheme.

Successful rehabilitation must necessarily involve popular participation of villagers to make the move an improvement in the standard of living, while maintaining cultural continuity. Various parks in India can learn from the early Kanha example managed by H.S. Panwar in the 70s, and the heartening example of three villages which have recently moved out of Melghat. The resettlement at Melghat has been so successful that other villages both inside and outside the park are clamouring for resettlement! Another successful case of resettlement in the making is that of the migrant Gujjars of Rajaji National Park. The resettlement at Gaindikhata and Pathri has been generous. And the Chilla and Hardwar ranges, vacated just a season ago, have already come alive with growing and less shy animal populations, perceptibly increased grass cover, and indeed, even greater water flow in the *raos* and *sots*. These examples are the models to emulate; there is no need to block resettlement and encourage habitat fragmentation through the seductively-named but misleading Tribal Rights Bill.

Panna at some 540 sq km is small compared to the other two Madhya Pradesh parks discussed. However, Panna is already de facto connected to two sanctuaries in the west going all the way to Jatashankar. The forested Vindhyan hill range extends virtually all the way to Sagar in the west (including the forests adjacent to Buxwaho, Bijawar, and the Hirapur forests of Chattarpur), and past Ajaigarh and Kalinjar to Ranipur Wildlife Sanctuary of U.P. in the north-east, so further extension is possible in this direction as well. The once-rich Shyamgiri forests of Nagod district (in the Vindhyas) could also be protected as an independent unit. A larger Panna could allow for the dispersion of wildlife generated by improved conservation in the core area. This would allow Panna to harbour much larger animal populations than it does currently. Village resettlements from the core area would also help, and it is reassuring to know that nearly a dozen villages are proposed to be relocated, starting with Pipartola, which has just moved. Already the largest animal population in Panna are found in the Hinauta range, now that it has been freed of cattle and insular village populations.

The above examples are not the only cases where large parks can be created in India. A complex in the south, including Nagarhole, Bandipur, Wyanad, Brahmagiri, Satyamangalam, Sigur, and Mudumalai, is a ready possibility; where management of the larger area as an integrated unit would be much more effective in combating poaching and managing tourist impact. This has previously been suggested by the Rodgers and Panwar study of 1988.

Two critical forest corridors which need urgent protection are the Rajaji-Corbett corridor in U.P. and the Mahananda-Buxa-Manas corridor spanning West Bengal and Assam. In both cases, the creation of wildlife corridors would allow for uninterrupted dispersion of animal population for more than 300 km. This would help protect the rich biodiversity of the Siwaliks and allow the flora to regenerate by permitting large mammal migration.

Perhaps, someday, the Ranthambhor Aravallis could be connected to the Kuno Palpur Park being created for lion translocation in Morena district across the Chambal river, as well as even to Madhav National Park. Larger parks could also be built around Pench (to include forests in Maharashtra), Bori and Satpura in M.P., Nagarjunasagar in A.P., Dudhwa in U.P., and Palamau in Bihar. Perhaps the new states created—Chhatisgarh, Jharkhand and Uttaranchal—would showcase Indravati, Palamau and Dudhwa parks respectively, as their most important conservation projects and tourism sites. The rump states of U.P. and Bihar can focus on heavily-poached parks like Dudhwa and Valmikinagar as their prime protected areas respectively.

With a half dozen large park complexes across India receiving strong scientific and management attention, at least key Indian animals and ecological processes can be protected. Perhaps a new category of conservation status would be needed for a few select interstate complexes—Ecosystem/ Biosphere Projects. Additional conservation efforts could then work at improving biogeographic coverage from among the other five hundred parks and sanctuaries.

A further opportunity to increase the sizes of selected parks is to develop parks and park management across national borders. How Valmikinagar National Park would benefit from sharing the strong management and tourism inflow from Chitwan National Park in Nepal! Greater cooperation between the park mangers at Chitwan and Valmiki would go a long way in reducing the large-scale trans-border poaching currently taking place at Dudhwa, Katerniaghat and Valmikinagar parks. Similarly, Dudhwa, Buxa, the Sunderbans, Kanchenjunga, and Manas, could all benefit from trans-border park management and cooperation between India, Nepal, Bhutan, and Bangladesh. Perhaps this idea could be undertaken as a project under the auspices of the South Asian Association for Regional Cooperation (SAARC). The development of a few international large parks would prove strong enough excuse to promote eco-development projects, as well as to augment tourism infrastructure around the parks. Such parks may also be able to access international funding and free up resources for more difficult and purely domestic parks.

A large national park in the public eye offers greater protection to wildlife. To a state government, in lieu of timber revenues, the park increase could be justified by the development of tourism. Tourism can be dispersed over the larger park area as has happened at Corbett Park. The creation and conservation of larger park complexes will then at least arrest the imminent possibility of the extinction of large mammals and representative biogeographic habitats. Of course, ideally India would conserve all protected areas well, but we have seen where such a policy has got us, with most

Indian protected areas reporting inadequate management resources and attention. The current policy of general and unfocused conservation will continue to suffer from a combination of poaching, grazing, encroachment, mining, dereservation, timber theft, terrorist takeover, and so on. There must be some examples in India where conservation laws are observed in toto, where benefits accrue to states and to local people, and which can serve as examples to build a successful conservation strategy.

Employment

Tourism can create a significant number of jobs outside a park. But not enough to absorb the vast pool from neighbouring villages and towns. What then for at least those who are disbenefitted by alienation from resources of neighbouring parks? A simple solution gleaned from experience the world over (witness South Africa and the Conservation Corporation) lies in private forests being raised on lands adjoining these parks. The raising of these forests would create employment as well as benefit wildlife, effectively increasing buffers for the protected areas. These lands could be misused for *shikar*, or shooting, but adjoining farmlands offer the same opportunity. Here is another role for wildlife tourism—private forests managed for tourism would generate far more revenue (and far less problems) in being used for tourism rather than for *shikar*.

The controversial issue of shikar or culling or 'legitimate sport by sportsmen', could be handled by letting private individuals/organizations offer *shikar* or legitimate sport on isolated forests, raised from ruin and degradation (to be certified by apolitical, environmentally-supportive committees to be set up for the purpose), or started from scratch. No one can then complain of the depletion of wildlife by legitimate *shikar*. If sport shooting raises revenues for the government, and introduced wildlife population actually increase (witness the healthy population of Indian animals and birds in Texas, where they have been introduced), then there is no reason not to allow it. There is nothing wrong with parting film stars and politicians from their money, if that money can be put to use. The alternative is the recurrence of illegal poaching. In Jodhpur, a Bollywood film star was caught poaching blackbuck. Predictably, he was not convicted, and the fickle public displeasure has vanished.

India's experience shows that poaching can be driven underground; poaching cannot be stopped. Can anyone in all honesty say that there is proportionately less *shikar* going on in India today (given depleted wildlife populations) than before the ban of *shikar*? Otherwise, with the ending of legitimate *shikar* in India in the 80s, game populations would have increased substantially in the old shooting blocks! Whether India is ready to allow legitimate, regulated sport shooting or not, is a debate for a wider audience, and for state governments such as Punjab, Maharashtra, and Rajasthan, which have their own views and rights on the issue, given farmers' lobbies against crop damage.

Anyone can buy or use a parcel of land and raise a forest. This would take 20 years. Here is a controversial suggestion, particularly in light of the experience of the wasteland development exercise in India, where lands have been given away indiscriminately to the politically connected, and diverted for non-forestry purposes. Degraded forest lands outside parks could be given on 20-year leases to a few, select private parties for rehabilitation and for the development of wildlife tourism (not *shikar*). These degraded forests could be raised in 5-10 years since the root stock is intact. The government could stipulate the employment of local people for tourism and forestry works. Private silviculture could employ as many people as Forest Department silviculture. Tribal and local population could be accommodated preferentially in such schemes. The renewal of leases, which would be monitored by vigilant outside experts, would be conditioned on the success of such projects in raising forests and generating employment. Rather than being used for harvesting timber, such forests could be used exclusively for the sustainable harvesting of non-timber minor forest produce and tourism. It is heartening to note that M.P. has been considering such a scheme.

As in all such schemes, transparency in the selection and regulation of the private parties is absolutely critical. Perhaps only those parties who are strongly capitalized, or who offer grants as part of corporate giving for rural development (again, to be monitored by the likes of environmentalists and auditing firms) could be considered. Locally influential people, landlords, and VIPs, and commercial NGOs could be simply excluded by the financial and operational commitments involved.

Tourism Helps

Tourism, while no doubt a nuisance for the forester, actually helps conservation. Tourism generates employment for guides, restaurateurs, hoteliers, local shopkeepers, mechanics, and so on. Further, tourism helps create a local constituency which is monitoring wildlife, and effectively patrolling roads, rest houses, and whole forest blocks. Guides get trained by park authorities. They become champions of conservation in their villages. A network of information is set up in adjoining areas about the main mammals and the health of the forest. Ecological information is disseminated outside the park. This is already happening at some parks such as Ranthambhor, Corbett, Bandhavgarh, Bharatpur, Panna, Kanha, Sariska and Nagarhole. These are the same parks about which information is most easily available and where poaching is immediately highlighted. Little information is available on the rampant poaching and timber theft variously at Palamau, Indravati, Satkosia Gorge, Chandaka, Katerniaghat, Suhelwa, Bhitarkanika, Valmikinagar, Simlipal, Bhimgarh, Hazaribagh, Nanda Devi, and Chandraprabha.

Tourists should be asked to pay fees in excess of the nominal ones currently being charged. This process has already begun at Corbett park where entry fees in 2002 alone generated Rs. 84 lakh. These fees should be earmarked into eco-development funds or park budgets for purchasing land in critical buffers and corridors. Such funds could also be used for rehabilitation of insular villages and for paying for crop damage. Further, these monies could be used to install radio communication networks for park management. India will soon be covered by a nationwide radio trunking network, which should cover many parks in its purview. Finally, such funds could help parks procure modern firepower to combat the poachers of today.

The park administration should immediately get out of tourist infrastructure and leave this to the private sector, websites, or state tourism departments. Else park directors will continue to spend more of their time booking accommodation for all and sundry VIPs. This would also release more funds from limited park budgets for the strengthening of invigilation and control. It is not clear what should be done to the government Forest Rest Houses, which are regularly used by assorted influential people and conservation celebrities. Should they be managed by state tourism authorities and customers charged appropriately? If so, the infrastructure would definitely be improved, though the clientele might have to be restricted by the size of the facilities.

The publication of educational materials and maps for tourists helps make parks more approachable and useful. In this regard, the maintenance of forest roads for wildlife viewing is not harmful. The same roads which are maintained for tourism, are also used by forest guards. To negate the problems from concentration, tourism should also be developed in the buffers to increase vigilance there and to take pressure away from the central attractions. Finally, tourism at each park should be restricted to its carrying capacity identified and publicized in advance, so there are no long queues at park entrances (and no black market for entry permits either!). This is similar to the Bhutan tourist system, where the annual number of tourists admitted is limited and publicized in advance. The idea of restricting economic scale would find sanction in Herman Daly's works (Daly, 1989; Daly, 1996). Ranthambhor and Corbett are attracting more and more wildlife lodges, well beyond the carrying capacity of the parks, while many other parks, of comparable value, continue to be ignored.

Celebrity Parks

No park or tiger 'belongs' to some local personality or Delhi celebrity conservationist. There should be no incidence of visiting celebrities who override park management for commercial interests. When animals are too frequently exposed to human beings, they lose their fear for people. After the first book has made him/her a celebrity on the party circuit, the purveyor of fashion moves to another animal collection. When the public spotlight turns away and the poachers return, the tamed animals are slaughtered.

All this is simply to say that conservation should not be allowed to become personality-based. Forest Rest Houses should not be managed for VIPs and their entourages. People desperate to see a tiger should be encouraged to go to our pathetic zoos (till they are dismantled, read on...). Forests and parks should not be managed for tiger viewing—no tiger baiting at Kanha or anywhere else. Visitors should be encouraged to ignore the tiger and think instead of beetles and ratels—less attractive animals to some, but equally important in the food chain! Defocusing the tiger may be a way of eliminating the non-serious MTV generation, far removed from the dedication of the early Indian naturalists such as Salim Ali, R.S. Dharamkumarsinhji, E.P. Gee, P.D. Stracey, and Fatehsinhrao Gaekwad.

Government policy and the serious media can help by down-playing the media-hype or toadying to self-styled instant celebrities with handlebar mustaches and great grey beards, who declaim from five-star Convention Halls about 'my tigers' or 'my park.' All this, when the humble villager, the private idealistic conservationist, and the field forester and professional official, are neglected, downgraded and marginalized, and tiger-poaching and habitat loss through crony-elitist celebrity policies poses a real danger to animal survival.

Eco-Development

The presence of a national park may help develop the local telephone network, power supply, water supply, rail connections, air connections, and so on. This is not intrinsically a bad thing. Local people may be told why the area is a focus of public investment, which should also include the development of animal husbandry, bee-keeping, cottage industries, and so on. The idea is to sell the park to the surrounding population. The park should be seen as a magnet for non-threatening, environmentally-sensitive development rather than an inhibitor. Well planned, generous, and participatory rehabilitation schemes, which are welfare-enhancing, should be seen as an opportunity to use the excuse of the park to enhance the quality of life of remote, forest-dwelling communities.

Unfortunately, most rehabilitation schemes have not

involved the input of the people concerned, unlike the highly successful Kanha resettlement and the ongoing Kuno-Palpur project where 23 villages have moved voluntarily. Consequently, rehabilitation schemes in Indian parks have largely stalled, and, spurred by all-to-critical and ill-interested environmental activists, the very notion of rehabilitation has acquired negative connotations. As if the unsustainable lifestyles of ever-burgeoning human and animal populations, such as those of the 'Van' Gujjars at Rajaji National Park are simply not deserving of change and improvement, even if relocation is to become participatory and generous, as it might under greater public scrutiny.

Park Management—Getting Indians Involved

Corporate or foundation sponsorship for selected parks is a possible method of raising funds for park infrastructure, insular village relocation, local employment generation, and land purchase for corridors. Sponsors to an 'Indian Wildlife Fund' could be given tax breaks, as would accrue to any charitable contribution in India, rights to publicize their sponsorship, as well as routine access to forest accommodation. Given the modest annual budget of Project Tiger, there should be no trouble in raising at least as much money from private initiatives every year.

Advertising presents many opportunities. Sponsors could publicize their contribution to conservation as part of their regular media advertising. Alternatively, they could donate part of the sales on any product to this conservation fund, such as various credit card companies are doing worldwide.

This might even help them lift sales on their products, and so help them contribute more. Finally, sponsors might purchase the rights to sell 'Corbett Tea,' 'Sunderbans Honey,' or 'Palamau Amla', with the revenues going to the respective parks. Distasteful as the thought of branding the names of our national parks might seem, it could raise revenues for conservation. Given the seriousness of India's conservation problems, and the fact that most of our forests won't see the next 20 years, this is a small aesthetic price to pay for conservation.

Private sponsorship could pay for annual prizes for forest guards who arrest poachers, compensation for crop damage and cattle killed by predators, and even forest and wildlife officials killed by poachers, as has recently happened in Palamau and Kaziranga, and vehicles for anti-poaching activities. Sponsors can motivate forest guards by providing employment to the relatives of those guards who are injured by poachers or those who lose their lives to poachers. Some private sector-type management practices of rewarding merit can also be instituted into normal park administration, which today often penalizes the ranger who makes reports of poaching or timber theft (the Sanctuary-ABN Amro and Venu Menon-WTI wildlife awards are doing just this). The adoption of resettled villages or villages exerting resource pressures on parks by private sponsors, under the aegis of the park authorities, could also go a long way to easing pressures on the forest administration. It is heartening to know that the Corbett Foundation in Ramnagar has actually started doing these very things.

Any relationship with corporations or foundations should

be started up centrally, either by the Wildlife Institute of India or Project Tiger. Further developments can take place locally. This is to ensure transparency and the regulation of the relationship at a senior level. Companies from a number of sectors like tea, coffee, tourism, airlines, hotels, as well as local manufacturing, could join up. Examples include the Ballarpur group (with extensive paper interests, and now, strong support for the Wildlife Preservation Society of India, which is doing pioneering anti-poaching work), Godrej (has been long associated with WWF-India), the Tata Group (the Tata Iron and Steel Company can support Dalma, just as Tata Tea supports Eravikulam in the south), Williamson and Magor (they protect the White-winged Wood Duck in Assam. In addition, they have gardens near Kaziranga, Manas, Jaldapara, Gorumara, and Buxa), Indian Hotels (Khajuraho hotel near Panna, Sawai Madhopur hotel near Ranthambhor, Sasangir Lodge near Gir), Indian Drugs and Pharmaceuticals Limited and Bharat Heavy Electricals Limited (plants at Rishikesh can adopt Rajaji forests, from which land was excised for them), East India Hotels (a heritage property coming up near Panna forest at Rajgarh Palace, Chattarpur, Vanyavilas in Sawai Madhopur), Indian Airlines, Jet Airways, Welcomegroup (Keoladeo Ghana is near their Agra hotel), the UB Group (which has apparently bought a game ranch in South Africa, since private forests are not possible in India), the Indian Tourism Development Corporation (lodge at Bharatpur), the Sandur Manganese Group, Xerox (the Kashipur plant is near Corbett), and so on...

All such monies raised should be constituted into an

endowment component and a project component. The former would be administered centrally (for example, by the Wildlife Institute of India in Dehradun), the latter locally by the park director and a local management committee comprising prominent citizens, conservationists, ecotourism operators, NGOs, representatives of the district administration, local corporates, scientists, academics, etc.

In similar fashion, local schools and colleges must be encouraged to develop strong connections with neighbouring parks. School children should be given concessional entrance and programmes arranged for them. School children may raise money with campaigns for park projects. School children in Delhi have just participated in a very effective campaign to reduce the use of firecrackers during the Diwali festival. Such energy by youngsters, supplemented by well-organized visits to parks rather than to zoos, could be effectively channelized to supporting conservation initiatives across the country.

Finally, the practice of appointing respected and locally-resident conservationists as Honorary Wildlife Wardens should be encouraged, to the extent that this supports park authorities. This was done in the 80s and had encouraging results in some parks with excellent work done by genuine naturalists till the usual political lobbyists and socialites took over. People with controversial antecedents, legal tangles, and conflicting tourism/property interests should be proscribed from these posts.

No Zoos in India

Most, if not all, zoological parks in India, are the most primitive torture chambers for the animals concerned. Zoos do not support a high standard of zoological research, breeding programmes, or scientific interpretation. There is little point in describing the pathetic and inhumane treatment to animals in Indian zoos. I could start with the attack of pariah dogs in the Bikaner zoo, which led to the death of all the blackbuck there, and go onto describe the ongoing teasing and poisoning of animals by visitors at the prestigious Delhi zoo. The death of 20 odd tigers in Bhubaneshwar by negligence some years ago is typical of the situation of zoos across India. A visit to an Indian zoo is not about nature education, as much as it is about the systematic and long-drawn out torture of rare animals for sadistic, voyeuristic, and ultimately, meaningless 'pleasure'. In a country where the public will protect the monkey and the cow, the same public will show complete apathy to the incarceration of a big cat in a small enclosure for its ravaged 'life.'

Animals need to be protected in the forest, *in situ*. Nature education takes young people to the forest. Nature education does not bring a degraded travesty of the forest to the city. As Aldo Leopold wrote a century ago, 'recreational development consists not of building roads into the wilderness, but of building inroads into the still unlovely human mind.'

What I propose is the re-development of valuable land taken up by our pathetic zoological parks to release vastly more funds for conservation than exist today. This proposal is fiscally sensitive; the state will be less burdened than by giving its measly conservation grants which do not account for even 10% of the annual Indian revenues from forestry.

Zoos may be redesigned, starting with Delhi, to release a combination of green space (beneficial for the town or city, and its residents, so that they are equitably compensated), and low-intensity institutional/office/commercial space. Sensitive urban development which also promotes Indian conservation could include a customized selection from Lodi Gardens, Dilli Haat, Apollo Hospital, Qutub Institutional Area, Coffee Home, and Indian Habitat Centre equivalents.

The funds that could be raised from selling the office/commercial/institutional space could dwarf the country's conservation budget for another 100 years! Managed as an endowment, the annual fund flow could even be diverted to perennially-strapped state governments in lieu of election-inspired, non-scientific forestry. Such is the quantum of capital tied up in these inhuman, dysfunctional and shabby organizations that serve little purpose and take up prime land in Indian cities. Besides, their annual budgets could also be saved, which by themselves would come close to that of Project Tiger. The funding released could solve the eco-development problems of all of India's parks, buy up lands for corridors, and easily fund park budgets.

Conclusions

The diverse suggestions made have some features in common. They are pragmatic rather than being ideologically motivated, involving greater participation by the Indian public for whom these areas are being managed. These solutions recognize the role of private enterprise and initiative (many forests in India have survived because they were once private property!), while reinforcing the need for a vigilant and transparent state system. These suggestions recognize the inevitability of faster economic development in India, which will bring both more destruction, and more affluence. This development cannot be stopped given the large population that India has to support; it can only be harnessed to minimize the environmental impact.

Economic theory (the Ricardian Theory of Rent) suggests that consumers (and governments) spend more in the present if they feel their revenues will increase in the future. The imperative for conservation stems from the same economic point of view. India will be prosperous in the future. A prosperous India can afford to save its forests and wildlife. Prosperous Indians will value wildlife. Hence India should invest in conservation today. This is an elitist view from the public point of view since scarce lands can be used for grazing and to produce food. However, since Indians of all walks of life invest in their children's education rather than harvest their labour, it is time we discarded this rejection of elitism and invested in a public good.

The ideological baggage of the last 50 years has to be rejected to accept elitist thinking on Indian conservation, just as it is accepted in justifying costly investments in Indian defense, space research, and technological development. These are investments undertaken by a poor country in order that it will not always be poor. True, funds are needed for investments in the social sector. These funds, critically needed in India, should come from the deconstruction of the

Indian state, which currently manages (for lack of a better word) almost half the economic assets of this country, ranging from the manufacturing of watches to the running of airlines. Just as the private sector must eventually take over these businesses which it can demonstrably manage better under transparent regulation, so must private initiative (scientifically and impartially regulated) be allowed to help the management of India's natural resources.

Leaving the management of India's protected areas outside the ambit of India's civil society, will continue the same decay and destruction that has been witnessed in all areas of Indian life which the Indian government system manages. The same Indian economic system, which is unable to deliver drinking water, health care or electricity, will not be able to deliver on a task as critical and complex as the conservation of India's still-rich biodiversity. I wonder how many Indians even know that the majority of Indian states (all save West Bengal, interestingly enough) routinely divert even the miniscule Central transfers for Project Tiger park salaries. [A telling foretaste of what will happen to the EGA!]. A Delhi NGO which took this matter to court, found that staff in parks like Kaziranga and Valmikinagar had arrears over a year apiece. Are we content leaving our natural heritage in such callously irresponsible hands?

Before questioning some of the aforementioned suggestions on involving private initiative in conservation, we must recognize where Indian conservation is at today. Orang and Pobitra Sanctuaries (where the Great Indian Rhinoceros is now extinct) in the state of Assam, and Gahirmata and Bhitarkanika Sanctuaries in the state of Orissa, have been actively settled with immigrants to build political votebanks. Manas National Park in Assam, a UNESCO World Heritage Site, is just limping back after having been taken over by insurgents and most large animals slaughtered. Kaziranga National Park has suffered from its annual floods, and animals seeking refuge in the neighbouring Karbi Anglong (formerly the Mikir North Cachar) hills, have been slaughtered, as per what is now an annual routine. Several thousand fresh immigrants have taken over parts of the Kaziranga buffer, and the courts, under pressure from local 'law-makers' have stayed resettlement efforts. Indravati National Park in Chhattisgarh, Valmikinagar National Park in U.P., and Palamau National Park in Jharkhand are the virtual preserve of terrorists, and the Forest Department, for all its professionalism and custodial efforts, has been made to lose control by the failure of governance of the Indian state. Developments in these outstanding forests now no longer even make the news. A third of Melghat National Park has recently been dereserved. Even a well-protected park like Corbett National Park has suffered from repeated Elephant poaching, apart from having a dam flood its priceless Core grasslands. The residents of the dam colony in Corbett haven't moved out after 20 years, despite court orders recently mandating their eviction!

Underlying all this destruction is the Indian political establishment, which will continue to settle immigrants on forest land and dereserve forest land for assorted ill-conceived industrial projects, instead of applying existing environmental regulations governing land use strictly and impartially. Regardless of election manifestoes, all democratic, electorally sensitive, political parties in India, will make the same transaction that took place in Orang and Gahirmata, and scores of wilderness locations all over India. It is sobering to realize that a quarter of Assam's still-rich forests are host to squatters, often themselves the fronts for already large local landlords. Which is why the upcoming Bill ostensibly framed for securing tribal rights in forests, promoted without debate, adequate safeguards, or any commitment to outcomes, will neither help with conservation nor bring development to forest-dwelling tribals.

After fifty years of Indian Independence it would be fitting if the Indian people (as distinct from the Indian state) finally assumed the responsibilities associated with their cherished democratic rights. The most precious Indian right to wilderness must be accompanied with growing public responsibility for its management.

5

Trail Guide—Places of Interest

Pandupol

Pandupol is a beautiful spot of mythological significance—it is believed the Pandavas spent part of their *Agyatvas* at this location. At Pandupol there is a 35-feet high waterfall arising from near the crest of the Aravalli ridge, where the deep fissure is said to have been created by Bhima. Short of the waterfall, which is accessible by road, there is an old Hanuman temple. The road leading to the temple is full of 'langurs', peafowl, spurfowl, and the ubiquitous tree pies. There is a large mela at Pandupol every year, attracting pilgrims from afar. Every Tuesday, pilgrims are permitted to drive through the park to visit this shrine.

Bhartrihari

It is said that the famous ruler of Ujjain, Raja Bhartrihari, spent his meditative years at this spot, 35 km from Alwar. The temple is situated at the edge of the forest, though the throngs of pilgrims undermine the pristine setting. Bhartrihari was a famous and enlightened ruler who abdicated when he realized the folly of material attachment (and philandering paramours!).

Narayaniji

This location hosts the famous Narayani Mata temple. There is a small *kund* located at the base of a slab of marble near the temple, which has water all year-round. Not far is the Baldeogarh fort in ruins.

Talvriksh

Talvriksh hosts a temple with hot and cold sources of water, about 35 km from Alwar, and very close to the park itself on the Narayaniji road. There is a grove of old ('arjun') trees, making this a picturesque spot. It is said that Mandavya rishi meditated at this spot.

Naldeshwar

Just off the main approach to Sariska from Alwar, Naldeshwar is an old Mahadev temple. The approach to the temple, surrounded by dense forests, requires a 2-km walk from the main road. Beyond Naldeshwar, is the fertile Naldi-Naldi valley, full of old 'jamun' trees.

Neelkanth Mahadeva

This is a complex of ancient temples on the Kankwari plateau, surrounded by a multitude of fallen carvings. The carvings resemble those built by the Chandelas of Khajuraho, and probably date to that time (9th-10th century A.D.). There are remains of nearly 340 dilapidated temples nearby, some of which are Jain shrines. Apparently, this was a capital of the Bargujars, who ruled Amber before the Kachhwahas. Alternatively, these could have been the work of the Gurjar-Pratiharas. The ASI has collected some statues in a 'museum,' but much archaeological work remains. A number of temples have already been demolished, and the *dhak* forest lands adjacent encroached. There is still a functional Shiva temple and a single giant statue of the 23rd Jain Tirthankar, locally known as 'Nogaza.'

Kankwari Fort

Just past the Tehla road, a track branches off to the north for Kankwari. Through dense forest on top of the Aravalli ridge, this track leads to an impressive view of Kankwari—a medieval fort on an isolated hill in the middle of a vast plateau. Kankwari has a *bandh* with perennial water. The fort has double crenallated walls reaching down to the water, surrounded as it is by a pure stand of 'khajur' trees. The western section of the plateau also hosts a couple of villages, surrounded by ever-widening circles of rack, ruin and degradation. Nothing can illustrate the influence of grazing more clearly than the sight of swathes of bare soil surrounding these villages.

Kankwari's claim to fame is the belief that Aurangzeb imprisoned Dara Shikoh here. A visit to the fort reveals an old well, a few old 'imli' trees, and royal residences on the upper parts, adorned by wall paintings of flowers. All the while affording the most imposing views of the plateau in all directions. If the isolated villages here were resettled, this could be the most productive forest in Sariska. This plateau is also accessible by the new metalled road running from Tehla and Neelkanth via Rajoregarh.

Ajaibgarh-Bhangarh-Pratapgarh

In Rajasthan it is natural to expect ruined forts at the edge of the forest. And so it is at Sariska. The most famous is Bhangarh, built in 1613 by Madho Singh, son of the great Mughal general, Man Singh of Amber. Bhangarh was abandoned soon after being built and offers an undisturbed view of the medieval past. Ajaibgarh is a beautiful garrison fort between Bhangarh and Pratapgarh, with a lovely reservoir nearby. The fort was built by Ajab Singh Rajawat, grandson of Madho Singh. The fort is in good condition, and affords a panoramic view of the eponymous walled town, the well-preserved, but disused temple (Shri Raghunathji), and old *chhatris*, all nearby. Apparently, the town had been depopulated by an old Mughal expedition, and is just reverting back to being habited again. Pratapgarh is an impressive hill fort which dominates the region.

Mangalsar *bandh*

Off the Tehla-Narayaniji road, this *bandh* is one of the largest in the region. The *bandh* attracts ducks/geese in winter.

Jaisamand *bandh*

Just 9 km from Alwar, this large *bandh* and its impounded waters, are home to a multitude of water birds. The *bandh* comprises a set of traditional *chhatris*, which make for a pleasant picnic destination. The *bandh* was made in 1910 by Maharaj Jai Singh.

Rajoregarh

The village of Rajoregarh, accessible from Tehla, hosts 9th century Siva temples, renowned for their craftsmanship and antiquity.

Siliserh and nearby

Just 16 km from Alwar, this large *bandh* and lake is a picturesque destination right at the edge of the Sariska park. The water that was impounded by this *bandh* in 1845 is spread over 10.5 sq km. On a clear day one can see crocodiles in the water, besides the usual complement of water birds (including geese in winter). Paddle boats can be hired to explore the waters. The Siliserh palace, built by Maharaja Vinay Singh for his queen Shila, must have been a fine monument to bygone days of shooting and pleasure. Today it is in shambles; the state cannot possibly maintain such a refined monument to bygone opulence. Beyond Siliserh, on the road to Bakhtpura village, there is a waterfall called Garwaji, which makes for an impressive sight in the monsoons. The walking track from Siliserh to Bala Qila should also be an interesting excursion through good forest.

Alwar town and its attractions

Alwar finds earliest mention in history as the capital of the Matsya Desh (1500 B.C.). The nearby town of Bairat (or Viratnagar) is supposed to have hosted the Pandavas for 13 years of their mythological exile. In more recent recorded history, Alwar changed hands between the Kachhawahas, Nikumbh Rajputs, Burgujars and Khanzadas (a clan of Meos founded by Bahadur Nahar). In 1775, Alwar was wrested from the Mughals by Pratap Singh and his Narukas of Amber. In 1803, Alwar state was founded with an endorsement by the emerging British power in India.

The principal destination for a tourist in Alwar is the **City Palace**, or **Vinay Vilas**. This palace was built in characteristic Rajput style the 18th century, and is predictably in a state of utter disrepair in the hands of the state. The lower floors house the Courts and the Collectorate. The museum is located in one upper apartment. The collection of the Alwar museum is truly outstanding, better than the permanent collection at the National Museum in Delhi. This small museum probably has the richest collection of Mughal and Rajput miniatures in India from the 18th and 19th centuries. In addition, there are precious manuscripts in Persian, Arabic, Urdu and Sanskrit. The major attractions are 'Gulistan' (the garden of roses, a treatise in Persian), 'Waqiate Babari' (Babar's autobiography) and 'Bostan' (poems). The museum also has a copy of the Mahabharata painted by the Alwar school. The collection of Indian weapons is also full of prize pieces, dating to Alwar's historical role both as a Mughal and a Rajput stronghold.

Right behind the Vinay Vilas is 'Sagar,' a large tank built by Maharaja Vinay Singh. Beside the tank is an impressive cenotaph of Maharaja Bakhtawar Singh, built in 1815. There is also a beautiful *chhatri* built to honour his consort—the Moosi Maharani. The tank urgently needs de-weeding and the *chhatris* aesthetic repair, to restore this rich complex to its rightful profile.

Company Garden (Purjan Vihar)

Another leading attraction is the Company Garden (Purjan Vihar) which was laid out in the town in 1868. The garden has a fernery called 'Simla,' built in 1885.

A visit to Alwar is incomplete without a meal at the Prem Pavitra Bhojanalaya near the old bus stand. This delightful restaurant offers the finest traditional vegetarian food cooked on a wood-fired hearth.

Alwar Fort (Bala Qila)

The famous fort is situated at a height of 595 m, 304 m above the town of Alwar. This fort, one of the few existing original Rajput forts, was built in the 10th century, making it a contemporary of Gwalior. The fortifications extend 5 km from north to south and 1.6 km from east to west, with ramparts extending 6.6 km. The fort has 15 large and 51 small towers. Eight major *burjs* or battlements defend this redoubt, along with 446 openings for musketry. Several large gates, named Jai Pol, Laxman Pol, Chand Pol, Krishan Pol and Andheri Gate enter the fort. The view from the heights is impressive, to say the least. There are numerous monuments at the high point—Jai Mahal, Nikumbh Mahal, Salim Sagar Pond (where it is suggested tigers used to come and drink in days past, though this would be difficult given the fortifications and gates), and Suraj Kund. The hilltop also boasts ancient temples to Hanuman. Bala Qila fort has hosted Babur, Akbar, and Jehangir—the last during a period of exile. Jehangir stayed here in the Salim Mahal.

Vijay Mandir Palace

This Royal retreat is situated to the north of the Bala Qila and 10 km from Alwar, on a picturesque road surrounded by forests. The palace, built in 1918, overlooks a large lake, and houses a temple of Sita Ram.

Bairat

Bairat is a small town located on the Alwar-Jaipur road with an abundance of history. The environs of Bairat boast pre-historic rock shelters, Ashokan edicts, an early Buddhist temple and associated monastery, early medieval temples, a pre-Mughal mosque, and a Mughal mint and garden. Between Bairat and Jaipur one passes through a picturesque range of forested Aravallis which might be revived some day, given that 'dhok' trees and leopards survive here gamely.

Accommodation

Inside the Reserve

There is a forest rest house at Sariska, located off the main Alwar-Jaipur road, beside the forest complex.

Contact: Field Director, Project Tiger, Sariska Tiger Reserve, P.O. Sariska, District Alwar 301001, Rajasthan [Tel (0144) 41333].

Outside the Reserve

The principal accommodation at Sariska is RTDC's newly-refurbished Tiger's Den, near the main gate of the park [Tel (0146) 2841342, 2841344].

Sariska Palace [Tel (0146) 524247, (011) 261888862; E-mail: sariska @del2.vsnl.net.in].

Tiger Haven is a new property developed nearer the Thana Ghazi park boundary.

There are many small hotels in Alwar, such as:

- RTDC Meenal [Tel 0144-2347302, 2334226]
- Aravali [Tel 0144-332883; Fax 0144-332011]
- Alwar [Tel 0144-220012; Fax 0144-332250]
- Jhankar [Tel 0144-23325510]
- RTDC Lake Palace [Tel 0144-86322]
- RTDC property (exquisite, but run-down) at Siliserh lake [Tel 0144-2286322, 2334266; Web: rajasthantourismindia.com]
- Amanbagh (newly-opened) near Ajaibgarh in the S.W. [Tel: +(65) 6887 3337; Fax: +(65) 6887 3338;

E-mail: info@amanresorts.com;
Web: www.amanresorts. com/bagh/home.htm]

- Hill Fort at Kesroli [Tel 0144-81312, 01468-289352; Delhi Tel (011) 24616145; Fax (011) 24621112; E-mail: sales@neemrana.com; Web: www.neemrana-hotels.com/kesroli/].

Bibliography

Ajith Kumar, C.R., and K. Sankar, 'Ichthyo-Fauna of Sariska Wildlife Sanctuary,' *Journal of the Bombay Natural History Society*, Vol. 90, p. 299-300, 1993.

Ali, Salim, and S. Dillon Ripley, *A Pictorial Guide to the Birds of the Indian Subcontinent* (Mumbai: BNHS, OUP, 1998).

Alves, J.P. Galhano and R. Garcia-Perea, 'Tigers and People: Strategies for Tiger Conservation in Sariska Tiger Reserve, India,' *CAT News*, 299-11, Autumn 1998.

Berkmuller, K.L., Mukherjee, S.K., Misra, B.K., 'Grazing and Cutting Pressure at Ranthambhor National Park,'(Dehradun, 1988), monograph.

Breeden, Stanley and Wright, Belinda, *Through the Tiger's Eyes—A Chronicle of India's Wildlife* (Berkeley, CA: Ten Speed Press, 1996).

Cairncross, Frances, *Costing the Earth* (London: The Economist Books, 1991).

Champion, H.G and Seth, S.K., *A Revised Survey of the Forest Types of India* (New Delhi: Government of India, 1968).

Centre for Science and Environment, 'Towards Green Villages: A Strategy for Environmental-Sound and Participatory Rural Development,' (New Delhi, 1989).

Colby, Michael, 'Environmental Management in Development: The Evolution of Paradigms,' (Washington, 1990), Discussion Paper, The World Bank.

Daly, Herman E., *Beyond Growth* (Boston: Beacon Press, 1996).

Daly, Herman E., *For the Common Good: Redirecting the Economy toward Community, the Environment, and a Sustainable Future* (Boston: Beacon Press, 1989).

Dang, Himraj, *Human Conflict in Conservation* (New Delhi: Har Anand Publishers, 1991).

Dang, Himraj, 'Conservations Thoughts,' *Seminar*, 71-74, April 1997.

Dang, Himraj, 'Parks versus People: The Challenge of Conservation in India,' *Parks*, 2 (3), 20-23, Nov. 1991.

Dang, Himraj and Hari Dang, in Watson, Alan E.; Aplet, Greh H.; Hendee, John C., comps. 2000. 'Conservation Thoughts from Central India,' *Personal, Societal, and Ecological Values of Wilderness*, Sixth World Wilderness Congress Proceedings in Research, Management, and Allocation, Vol. II, 1998.

Davidar, E.R.C., *Cheetal Walk* (New Delhi: Oxford University Press, 1997).

Dharamkumarsinhji, R.S., *Reminiscences of Indian Wildlife* (New Delhi: Oxford University Press, 1999).

Ewans, Martin, *Bharatpur Bird Paradise* (New Delhi: Lustre Press, 1989).

Goodland, Robert, 'Balancing Conversion with Conservation in World Bank Projects,' *Environment*, 31 (9), 7-35, Nov. 1989.

Goodland, Robert, 'The Environmental Implications of Major Projects in Third World Development,' *Major Processes and the Environment*, Chester, P., 1989.

Goodland, Robert, 'Tropical Moist Deforestation: Ethics and Solutions,' (Washington, 1990).

Gregersen, Hans, Sydney Draper, and Dieter Elz (eds.), 'People and Trees: The Role of Social Forestry in Sustainable Development,' (Washington, 1989), EDI Seminar Series, The World Bank.

Guha, Ramachandra (ed.), *Nature's Spokesman—M. Krishnan and Indian Wildlife* (New Delhi: Oxford University Press, 2000).

Gujarat Ecological Society, *Rare and Endangered Plants and Animals of Gujarat* (Vadodara: GES, 2003).

Hough, John L. and Mingma Norbu Sherpa, 'Bottom Up vs. Basic Needs: Integrating Conservation and Development in the Annapurna and Michiru Mountain Conservation Areas of Nepal and Malawi,' *AMBIO*, 1990.

Israel, Samuel, and Toby Sinclair (eds.), *Indian Wildlife Sri Lanka Nepal* (Hong Kong: Apa Productions, 1987).

Johnsingh, A.J.T., K. Sankar, and Shomita Mukherjee, 'Saving Prime

Tiger Habitat in Sariska Tiger Reserve,' *Cat News*, 27, 12/5/01.

Kanjilal, U.N., *Forest Flora of the Chakrata, Dehradun and Saharanpur Forest Division* (Dehra Dun: Natraj Publishers, 2004).

Karanth, K. Ullas, *The Way of the Tiger* (Bangalore: Centre for Wildlife Studies, 2001).

Kiss, Agnes (ed.), 'Living with Wildlife: Wildife Resource Management with Local Participation in Africa,' (Washington, 1990), The World Bank.

Kothari, Ashish, Singh, Neena, and Suri, Saloni, *People and Protected Areas—Towards Participatory Conservation in India* (New Delhi: Sage, 1996).

Kutty, Roshni, and Kothari, Ashish (eds.), *Protected Areas in India—A Profile* (Pune: Kalpavriksh, 2001).

Mathur, V.B., 'Ecological impacts of livestock grazing on wild ungulates in Sariska National Park, India,' IVth International Rangeland Congress, Montpellier, France, 1991.

McNeely, Jeffrey A., Kenton R. Miller, Walter V. Reid, Russell A. Mittermeier, Timothy B. Werner, 'Conserving the World's Biological Diversity,' (Washington, 1990), IUCN, WRI, CI, WWF-US, and the World Bank.

McNeely, Jeffrey A., 'How Conservation Strategies Contribute to Sustainable Development,' *Environmental Conservation*, 17 (1), 9-3, Spring 1990.

McNeely, Jeffrey A., 'How to Pay for Conserving Biological Diversity,' *Ambio*, 18 (6), 308-13, 1989.

Misra, Hemanta, 'A Delicate Balance: Tigers, Rhinoceros, Tourists and Park Management vs. the Needs of the Local People in Royal Chitwan National Park, Nepal,' in *National Parks, Conservation and Development*, eds. Jeffrey A. McNeely and Kenton R. Miller, (Washington: Smithsonian, 1984).

Menon, Vivek, *A Field Guide to Indian Mammals* (New Delhi: Dorling Kindersley, 2003).

Monga, Sunjoy, *Wildlife Reserves of India* (Mumbai: India Book House, 2002).

Panwar, H.S., 'Protected Areas and People—The Indian Approach,' *Proceedings of the 25th Working Session of National Parks and Protected Areas* (IUCN, May 1985).

Panwar, H.S., 'What to Do When You've Succeeded: Project Tiger Ten Years Later,' in *National Parks, Conservation and Development*, eds. Jeffrey A. McNeely and Kenton R. Miller, (Washington: Smithsonian, 1984).

Parmar, P.J., A Contribution to the Flora of Sariska Tiger Reserve, Rajasthan, *Botanical Survey of India*, Jaipur, Vol. 27, Nos. 1-4: p. 29-40, 1985.

Poffenberger, Mark, 'Joint Management of Forest Lands,' (New Delhi, 1990), The Ford Foundation.

Poole, Peter, 'Developing a Partnership of Indigenous Peoples, Conservationists, and Land Use Planners in Latin America,' (Washington, 1989), The World Bank.

Ranjitsinh, Dr. M.K., *Beyond the Tiger* (New Delhi: Brijbasi, 1997).

Rich, Bruce *Mortgaging the Earth: The World Bank, Environmental Impoverishment, and the Crisis of Development* (Boston: Beacon Press, 1994).

Rodgers, W.A., 'A Preliminary Account of the Vegetation of Sariska Tiger Reserve, Rajasthan,' Oct. 1985, unpublished note.

Rodgers, W.A., and Panwar, H.S., *Planning a Protected Areas Network in India* (Dehradun: WII, March 1988) in two volumes.

Rodgers, W.A., 'A Preliminary Ecological Survey of Algual Spring, Sariska Tiger Reserve, Rajasthan,' *Journal of the Bombay Natural History Society*, 87, 201-209, 1989.

Rodgers, W.A., '*Capparis sepiaria* L: An Important Dry Season Fodder Plant for Wildlife,' *Range Mgmt. & Agroforestry* 11(2): 199-206, 1990.

Ross, Caroline and Arun Srivastava, 'Factors Influencing the Population Density of the Hanuman Langur (*Presbytis entellus*) in Sariska Tiger Reserve,' *Primates*, 35(3), 361-367, July 1994.

Saini, K.L., 'Tiger Project,' unpublished note.

Saharia, V.B., 'Human Dimensions in Wildlife Management: The Indian Experience,' in *National Parks, Conservation and Development*, eds. Jeffrey A. McNeely and Kenton R. Miller, (Washington: Smithsonian, 1984).

Saharia, V.B., *Wildlife in India* (Dehradun: Natraj, 1982).

Sahni, K.C., *The Book of Indian Trees* (Mumbai: BNHS, OUP, 1998).

Sankar, K., Mohan D., and S. Pandey, 'Birds of Sariska Tiger Reserve,

Rajasthan, India,' *Forktail*, 8, 133-141, 1993.

Sekhar, N.U., 'Crop and Livestock Depradation Caused by Wild Animals in Protected Areas: The Case of Sariska Tiger Reserve, Rajasthan, India,' *Environmental Conservation*, 25(2), 160-171, 1998.

Sharma, Dr. Devdatt, *Bagh Pariyojna, Sariska* (Alwar: Sandarbh Prakashan, February 1988).

Sharma, D. and S.N. Prasad, 'Tree Debarking and Habitat Use by Porcupine (*Hystrix indica* Kerr) in Sariska National Park in Western India,' *Mammalia*, 56 (4), 351-361, 1992.

Sharma, V.D. and Rajpal Singh, *Wild Wonders of Rajasthan* (New Delhi: Prakash, 1998).

Soni, R.G., 'Tiger Returns to Rajasthan,' (Delhi, 2002), TCP.

Viksat, 'People's Involvement in Wildlife Management,' (Ahmedabad, 1991).

Wells, Michael, Katrina Brandon, and Lee Hannah, 'People and Parks: An Analysis of Projects Linking Protected Area Management with Local Communities Washington,' (Washington, 1990), The World Bank.

'Ziddi,' Dr. Suraj, *A Guide to the Wildlife Parks of Rajasthan* (Jaipur: Photo Eye Publications, 1998).

Index